W9-ABY-602

Black Self-Determination

Edited by

Robert F. De Haan, *Great Lakes Colleges Association*
Director, Philadelphia Urban Semester

Roberta G. De Haan

Black Self-Determination

The Story of The Woodlawn Organization

by

ARTHUR M. BRAZIER

WILLIAM B. EERDMANS PUBLISHING COMPANY
GRAND RAPIDS, MICHIGAN

Library of Congress Catalog Card Number: 77-78021

Printed in the United States of America

Foreword

The message of this book is simple. Black Americans must enter the mainstream of American life now. The nation must choose between democracy and repression, between the republic and a police state; for America cannot keep down thirty million people who are moving up, without destroying the entire nation in the process.

In order to enter the mainstream, black Americans must acquire power through organization. They must organize for their basic self-interests. They must organize in order to find their own identity, dignity, and destiny. They must organize to keep from being exploited or helped in paternalistic ways by white society. Only then will people of color be powerful enough to claim a rightful place in American life.

When black people organize, white people panic and strike back. White society will not relinquish the power with which it has held the black man in his "place" for almost four hundred years—not without fighting every step of the way. History has shown that black people cannot rely on the moral integrity of organized white society to give power to black people voluntarily. It must be wrested from that society. The price of acquiring power is conflict and confrontation; but neither need be violent. Black Americans must seize the right and power of self-determination now.

There are two facets to this problem. Black people need a way out of the ghetto into an open society in which they can freely move, and they need control over their life situation within their community wherever they are.

Black people must reject everything negative the white man has said about them. Every sign and hint of racial superiority in the thinking of whites must be denounced by blacks. White men dragged the black man to this country against his will, stripped him of his African heritage, gave him a nondescript name, called him a Negro instead of an African, called him a boy instead of a man, rejected his racial characteristics, imposed a servile personality on him, and coerced him into believing he was inferior. Blacks cannot allow this fantastic myth of white superiority to influence them any longer. They must identify with blackness, see that black is good, generate pride in religion, culture, family, race. People of color need not prove their equality at the bar of white justice; they can claim it as a historical fact.

The time is here for black people in America to organize the black community from within for self-determination. Without this organizing and the power that grows from it the black man will not be able to enter the mainstream. The black community at the present time faces two problems with organization. It is organized from the outside by white society for the political and economic interest of whites. It is splintered from within by a multitude of organizations that have only fragmentary influence but no real power. Black men must make united, organized efforts to deal with every facet of their own interests in the face of resistance from the Establishment outside and from narrow divisive forces inside.

A myriad of local groups take the first step toward organization, and then get bogged down in their own inertia. A total organization must be set in motion having the strength to go on to take the second, the fifth, the twentieth step. This book is largely about how one black community took such steps and what it is doing for the future.

In this the church has a role to play. The church led the way in understanding and implementing the struggle of the black man for identity, dignity, and self-determination in Woodlawn. Withdrawal of the church into a purely spiritual ministry is indefensible, especially from a biblical Christian view. To do nothing is to take sides with the Establishment in maintaining the oppressive status quo against the black community. By positively affirming the rights and the gifts of the black man and by helping him take effective action, the church can underscore the preaching of the gospel of salvation in Christ by responsible living in Christ.

Contents

Chapter One

Powerlessness to Power

Few people outside its boundaries understand life in the ghetto. To most outsiders the ghetto is an unpleasant amorphous abstraction—perhaps only a memory of some documentary film on inner-city problems, a sterile research report on life styles of the poor, a second- or third-hand experience from a speaker at a club or church meeting. Although a few outsiders have toured the ghetto, the typical middle-class white person does not conceive of ghetto life in terms of people.

This book talks about the ghetto in terms of people—real people who have families, neighbors, children, homes, churches. It talks about their frustrations, the indignities heaped upon them. Above all it speaks about their drive for self-determination. That drive is gaining momentum. It is one of the signs of real hope for the black people of ghetto America.

The writer is pastor of the Apostolic Church of God, a church in the Woodlawn area; he is also an officer in The Woodlawn Organization. He sees, hears, smells, and touches the life of the ghetto. There is a young mother of three small children living in a one-room apartment. More than half her welfare check goes for rent, the rest for food. When the heat is turned off or the plumbing collapses or the plaster falls off the walls she has no power to correct the situation. Her children already look at their inhospitable little world with blank, uncomprehending eyes. There are groups of children roaming the streets aimlessly, kicking empty beer cans, throwing sticks and stones at the buildings that seem to confine them in the ghetto. Young children still laugh and play, but older ones are silent and sullen.

There are few tall residential buildings in the community, and land coverage by buildings is very great. For most of its history Woodlawn has been a built-up community with extreme deficiencies in yard space, parking, play and recreational areas. The United States census of 1960 indicates that somewhat more than 60,000 persons live within the area of a little less than one square mile that makes up Woodlawn, with a net density of almost 250 persons per acre. This makes Woodlawn one of the most densely occupied communities in Chicago.

Housing in Woodlawn has been progressively deteriorating for years, since before black people moved in. Fifty percent of the housing units in the area are dilapidated, deteriorated, or deficient in basic plumbing facilities. Almost 27 percent of these housing units contain more than one person per room, compared with less than 12 percent for the rest of the city, according to the 1960 census.

Somewhere out in the suburbs sits a white man who collects rents from these properties, through one or more fronts. He manipulates the legal structures of society so he can continue to pile up money from his almost uninhabitable slum housing. He does not think of people when he thinks of the ghetto.

Who in the white community has smelled the foul odor of uncollected garbage in the halls of ghetto apartments? In Woodlawn those garbage heaps convey the stench of hopelessness. People eat spoiled meat and bad vegetables, food that should have been consigned to the dump heap. There are enough unscrupulous merchants who lie, overcharge, and underweigh in the ghetto, however, to keep people not only helpless but hopeless as well.

Young people from the ghetto offer their high school diploma to a potential employer expecting it to show their credentials for a job, but then they fail to pass a simple employment test that any high school graduate ought to be able to pass. The school system produces functional illiterates and leads them into believing they are employable.

The ghetto schools are financed, administered, and largely taught by white people who continue to educate ghetto children as if they came from typical middle-class homes with all the intellectual and cultural enrichment such children receive. This is not to say there are no cultural resources in black family life. The school system, however, does not tap the cultural resources of the black community when it establishes its curriculum. To blame a ghetto mother for not stimulating her children so they can learn is not only futile, it is cruel as well.

What happens to young people, particularly young men, whom the schools have failed to prepare to enter the world of work? They hang around the street corners in sullen little groups. They form the "hard-core unemployables." Their spirits smolder; desperation mounts to the point where lashing out against the world in angry riots is the only alternative to shriveling up and dying inside.

These youth form their own organizations, which outsiders call gangs, in which they seek to attain legitimate ends by sometimes illegitimate means. While one cannot endorse illegitimate or illegal activity, one must say that a group structure that sustains their personhood is better for our youth than having the light of personhood die out of their eyes altogether in a hopeless struggle against cruel odds.

This is Woodlawn, on the central south side of Chicago—a square mile packed with human beings, bounded by 60th Street on the north, Stoney Island on the east, Cottage Grove Avenue on the west and 67th Street on the south. Woodlawn is a neighborhood that has absorbed thousands of immigrants from the south who poured out of the 63rd Street Station of the Illinois Central Railroad while the rest of Chicago stood by and let the neighborhood collapse. It is a neighborhood where streets still hold last winter's salt and last fall's leaves in the gutters, where boarded-up shop windows speak to the residents of the white man's racism, where spray-paint graffiti on buildings and fences remind everyone of the explosive mixture of hope and suppressed rage to be found in every young person who roams the streets.

Entry into the Mainstream

Black people, both young and old, know there is a better world, better jobs, decent housing, good schools, recognition as human beings. Black Americans in the ghetto know how affluent Americans live and they want to share that affluence. This revolution of rising expectations is the change that is going on in the black ghetto now.

Most white Americans believe it is exclusively the efforts of the white man that have made America great and affluent. The Protestant ethic of work, save, rise, and succeed is supposed to be the foundation on which the American dream is built. Black people know this is a half-truth. They know that America was built on the backs of the black man. They know that the black man's role in the history and in the success of America has never been acknowledged, that the black man has never received the due reward of his labor. While he grew cotton, he was ill clad. Although he built the railroads, he was refused a seat on them. A black medical doctor discovered blood plasma but died because he could not get a transfusion.

Black Americans want in—now! They want full and equal participation in all phases of American life. They are not going to leave America. They are not going back to Africa to set up a little reservation; they have too great a stake in this land. Great progress has been made for a relatively few blacks, but for millions of others the American dream is getting farther out of reach every day. While wealth piles up in selected areas of society, poverty holds unrelenting sway in other areas. The ghetto must find access to the mainstream. The poor are demanding redress and their black brothers are speaking for them.

Today many Americans are more concerned about law and order than they are about justice and mercy. Black people too want law and order. But at what price? At the price of classifying protesters and demonstrators with criminals and hoodlums as lawbreakers? At the price of setting up machine guns on every corner to keep the ghetto citizens in their place? At the price of giving every policeman the right to frisk anyone he chooses, to shoot suspected looters on the spot, to act as judge, jury, and executioner?

Whites may agree to use police-state methods to control the ghetto, thinking all the while that such tactics will never be used against them. They should read the lesson of recent history. The Jews in Germany were rich and powerful in the early days of Hitler's regime. They failed to see the danger they were in as his police state developed, and when it was too late the police state turned on them.

Once police-state methods become accepted as the way things are done, no one is immune. Which group would next be considered undesirable? Who would next need to be controlled? The mentality of law and order at the expense of justice and mercy soon hardens the mind to violence, twists the conscience, perverts the sense of values. Many people applauded the police clubbing of students, newsmen, and bystanders at the 1968 Democratic Convention in Chicago. If America follows that course, no one will ever be free in this land again.

The revolution of rising expectations was first expressed in slogans such as FREEDOM NOW and WE SHALL OVERCOME! People of color now speak of BLACK POWER and SELF-DETERMINATION—not as a threat of violence, but as a shout of self-confidence and ability to change things. For organized white society to keep the black man out of the mainstream of American life, or to harass him as he makes his way in, simply will not work. There are too many black men wading in. The black community is on the move.

History of Powerlessness for Black Men

The Afro-American, unlike the white immigrant, was rooted out of his home in Africa against his will and transplanted to this country. Here he was stripped of his African tradition, heritage, history. Dispersed among Southern plantations he lost his tribal identity, his regional affiliations, his family ties. During the long nightmare of chattel slavery the black man was stripped of all power and human dignity. He could own no property, he could enter into no contract, he had no standing in court, he could not meet with other black men in public unless there was a white man present. If a slave tried to think independently or acted in any way that could lead his master to think he was "uppity," he was quickly turned over to a white person called a slave breaker.

After Emancipation and the Civil War, the black man found that although he was free from the physical abuse of the slave master and the humiliating status of chattel slavery, he was a victim of another kind of slavery just as humiliating and diabolical. He found himself in the iron grip of economic and political slavery, which for a hundred years would relegate him to the position of menial servitude not much above the slavery he had just escaped.

The black man's position of powerlessness in the South was increased by the enactment of laws that officially segregated the blacks and gave legal sanction to racial discrimination. In 1896 the Supreme Court approved "separate-but-equal" facilities, and segregation became an established fact. Racial segregation and discrimination were carried out so vigorously that the black man was completely alienated from the mainstream of American life. The enactment of Poll Tax laws and the threat of physical violence kept black people from voting. Even though blacks composed a large part of the Southern population, and in many Southern counties actually outnumbered the whites, there were no elected officials who were nonwhite, from the governor of the state down to the sheriffs in the local counties.

The absence of political power of the black people in the South had its effect upon them in the courts. The black man could not get legal redress from his grievances in the Southern courts, especially if his complaint was against a white man. Being held in a position of utter powerlessness, the black man became a prey for every person or group who desired to exploit him; and unquestionably the black man was exploited to the utmost.

The first great migrations of blacks from the rural South to the urban areas of the nation came during World War I. This mass migration was in response to the Northern industrialists' urging the black people to come north to find better jobs. In response to this propaganda and to escape the abuse of poverty and the exploitation of the South, the Afro-Americans migrated north in large numbers, searching for a better life for themselves and for their children. The North, however, was not prepared for this great movement, and during this period began the formation of what have now become the great black ghettos of the nation.

Many Northern cities, in order to contain the black man in specific geographic limits, set up what has become known as the restrictive covenant, whereby a buyer agrees not to sell the property to a black man if he moves later. This legal artifice had the sanction of law until it was declared unconstitutional by a Supreme Court decision in 1948. One of the Northern cities that capitalized on the restrictive covenant was the city of Chicago. Chicago became so blanketed by restrictive covenants that it was known throughout the country as the most segregated city in the nation.

Having come to the North, the black man was lulled into a sense of false security, because he saw a difference between the attitude of the Northern white man and that of the Southern white man. The Southern white man openly abused the Afro-American and let him know in no uncertain terms that he considered him an inferior human being. The Northern white man acted out his prejudices in a much more civil and sophisticated manner.

The potential political power of large numbers of black people concentrated in the industrial cities of the North increased a good deal. But the black people in the North, having been historically denied the right to go to the ballot box in the South, did not have the political sophistication to vote effectively. They were politically exploited by both the Republicans and the Democrats.

The position of economic powerlessness, however, remained unchanged during this beginning of change in political position. In the city of Chicago, for example, black people were relegated to the most menial jobs. Systematic and conspiratorial job discrimination was rampant. During the 1930's, a black man could not get a job driving a Yellow or a Checker Cab. He could not get a job as a motorman or a conductor on the Chicago Surface Lines, nor on the Chicago Rapid Transit System. He could not get a job as a bus driver for the Chicago Motor Coach Company. Practically all of the big utilities and large industrial complexes refused to give a black man a job, other than pushing a broom or washing windows or shining door knobs at the public entrances.

Craft unions were especially vicious in barring blacks from their ranks. This well-organized effort to prevent black people from getting decent jobs was so effective that at one time the elite of black society was made up of pullman car porters, dining car waiters, and government employees in the Post Office.

Political exploitation took such forms as appointing a black man to a specific office. The mayor of a city would appoint a black person as a director or deputy director of something or other. Seeing this appointment being made, the people in the ghetto would say that "the mayor is all right" because he appointed a black man to an office. This was misleading, however, because although the appointed black man did have a good job and dealt with whites on an apparently equal level, yet he himself had no power. He took orders from the man who appointed him. This appointed black person would, in many cases, be a front Negro who would always stand up for the particular administration that appointed him and speak in favor of it. This had the effect of lulling the black masses into a sense of being represented where in fact they were not.

The black man's political and economic powerlessness has had a tremendous effect on the lives of his children, especially in their education. Black children have not been adequately educated. Education in the ghettos has become little more than a holding action until the black child is old enough to drop out of school. The inferiority of most ghetto schools is well documented—classrooms are overcrowded in black neighborhoods; schools where black children attend often have the least-experienced teachers; less money is spent in black schools; what they are taught has little relevance to their present or future lives.

The lack of political and economic power has also affected the black person in his relationship with law-enforcement agencies. It is again well documented that there is more police brutality in black neighborhoods than in white neighborhoods. Certainly not every policeman in a black community abuses his power. The majority of them in fact do not. Enough of them, however, do go beyond the limits of their power and authority—enough of them do verbally and physically abuse black people—that there has grown a deep alienation between certain sections of the black community and the police force.

In both the North and the South, then, the black man in America has been, for the most part, economically, politically, and educationally powerless.

To some degree black people must share the blame for their own exploitation. Many blacks have not taken advantage of their voting power by electing officials who would represent their aims and their aspirations. Black people in Chicago have too long depended on the precinct captain to tell them how to vote and for whom to vote. They have too long trooped to the polls and dutifully voted the straight party ticket regardless of whom the party slate-makers put on the ticket. Black people have failed to organize and utilize their "people power" for their own self-interest. Black people must get themselves together.

Integration of blacks as a group into white society is now being recognized as an impossible achievement in the present state of affairs. Further, blacks no longer need to find their identity by association with whites, as is implied by integration. They can do so now in terms of their own blackness. Instead of spending enormous amounts of energy on trying to integrate large bodies such as the Kiwanis Club, unions, whole neighborhoods, black people should concentrate on forming their own quality organizations. This is happening in many places in the country. Black teachers are forming their own unions, black policemen their own associations, black transit workers their own groups. At this time integration of white organizations usually only means that the black man will remain outnumbered and in an inferior position, because the dominant white membership will decide how many blacks will be integrated and on what terms. The white membership still holds the power and will decide the policies.

Although there are those who believe group integration is an achievable goal at this time, the facts seem to indicate otherwise. Twenty years after the U.S. Supreme Court outlawed restrictive covenants, fourteen years after the Supreme Court struck down school segregation, long after the Chicago Summit Meeting between Martin Luther King and the mayor and the Chicago Real Estate Board as well as most of the other power structures of the city, years after pledges were made to black people that Chicago would work for an open city, Chicago remains one of the most segregated cities in the United States. In spite of all the legislation and promises, segregation increases as the black population increases.

The integrated community is, for the most part, a myth, an act of wishful thinking. Whatever amount of integration has been achieved in schools has occurred only by periodic gerrymandering of school districts. The idea of group integration is still promoted by well-intentioned efforts of groups and interracial committees who involve themselves in promoting brotherhood weeks, writing resolutions, and passing out testimonials and awards—all of which have no meaning or effect upon the masses of black people who are struggling for survival.

The solutions to the problem must be implemented at the same time. Black people must build up their own communities and make them desirable places to live, work, play, and send their children to school. This means encouraging people to remain in their community and helping them improve the quality of living in it. All communities work toward the same end of making their place a desirable place for them and their children. At the same time Americans must also establish widespread opportunities for individual integration in housing and in jobs, so that a person can move where he chooses or get a job wherever he is qualified.

To build up their own communities black Americans must acquire power. The need is not for slogans and rhetoric, but for mass-based organizations that can develop the kind of power necessary within the black community to change the domination of white power structures that continue to exploit black people.

Black Power

The words "black power" articulate three major feelings: (1) pride in color, (2) self-determination, and (3) a clear recognition that some form of power organization is necessary to open up the country to the black race. To understand the real concept of power one must understand the principles, practices, and purposes of organization. Without organization there is no power, only talk.

When powerless people begin to demand power and self-determination they generate within themselves a real sense of dignity that demands respect. Where there is no respect, there is no real understanding and no love. Love is a word that is bandied about a good deal today. When people begin to respect each other as human beings, then and only then is there opportunity for love to develop. This is the relationship between power and love. Power brings about the conditions whereby respect and dignity can be obtained so that love can grow out of that respect and that dignity.

The word "dignity" is very important. Dictionary definitions of the word such as "worthiness," "nobility," "self-posession," "self-respect" are not enough. The word means these things and more. It must be defined in terms of free will and self-determination. A person who does not have free will loses respect for himself and has no dignity, because he knows people are using him and manipulating him. Out of this lack of self-respect and dignity a person begins to act in antisocial and violent ways. He has nothing to lose.

The loss of dignity is, in reality, the loss of that which God has given man in the first place. Man is a self-determining creature. This is a part of what the Scriptures mean by saying he is made in the image of God. Man is a moral being: he has the ability to choose right or wrong. He has the desire also to determine what to do with his person. The lack of self-determination is in part what made slavery so abominable. Even though a slave sometimes lived in the home of a perfectly loving master, that master was in control of the slave's destiny. Freedom today means that people of color must turn their backs on even the most benevolent paternalism and make their own way. Only then will they be a self-determining people.

To accomplish this, citizens must participate in the decision-making process as it relates to them. Self-determination is essential to the entire democratic process. Citizen participation calls for a means, a mechanism whereby the desires of the people can be made known. Through this mechanism, this organization, citizens can change the conditions in which they live. This is power.

Black Americans now understand that fundamental changes can take place only when the people who are outside the Establishment make demands upon the Establishment. Meaningful change can only come about when there is a crisis situation. People outside the Establishment must confront the Establishment with a crisis situation and seize upon it so that relevant change can be brought about. The only way for black people to bring this about and to get their fair share of the affluence of America is through a power organization. This organization need not be disorderly or violent, only powerful. The Woodlawn Organization has shown that there can be an orderly revolution operating within the framework of American democracy. Power is not corrupt in itself. The persons who seem to warn everyone against power, and who seem to feel that it is a most sinister and corrupt commodity, are the persons who have power and who wield it effectively for their own ends.

Organizational Power

Organizations should not be afraid of power. They should see power for what it is and use it. A community organization, to operate on a base of power, must be oriented to action. The problem of power as related to action is a simple one: one has to ask what ends are to be achieved and what means are available and most effective. Power is the means to achieve goals.

Rent strikes are an example. No one likes a strike. Yet a strike is an exercise of power. If sitting down at the bargaining table does not bring about the goal of an equitable solution and the only instrument available is a strike, then a strike must be used.

If a community organization tries to negotiate with a slum landlord and finds that every appeal to reason is of no avail, that every appeal to do what is morally right falls on deaf ears, then it is proper that this organization should resort to a rent strike to bring the landlord to the place where his own self-interest is jeopardized. Then he will sit down at the bargaining table and begin to negotiate.

A power-based community organization must also bring about confrontation and conflict. Where there is no controversy, there is no issue. It is only when two groups or two people disagree that the issue is drawn. No vital community organization can exist without controversy. And this controversy must not be limited to one issue but must take up a multiplicity of issues.

A strong community organization, run by the people and for the people, possesses the confidence of the people. It is a community organization whose end is improved living conditions and not mere talk. A community organization that believes in action is not the kind of community organization described by Saul Alinsky as "still-born corpses identified with a letterhead." It is not just holding one more annual meeting concerned with new horizons in community organizations. It is a strong action-oriented organization in which people find their own dignity because the organization does not beg but negotiates with the Establishment as an equal.

A power organization should not be simply a civil rights movement or simply a slum-housing movement or simply a movement against police brutality. A power organization should be all these things and more. To do the many things that must be done simultaneously in the ghetto requires organized power. The question is not whether we shall overcome, but whether the power structure is going to come over—with jobs, improved educational approaches, adequate housing, a more enlightened approach to the welfare problems.

Black people must always remember that equality and freedom are two things that will never be handed to them on a silver platter. These things will not come as an act of charity or as an act of good will. When they have the strength to take them, and by the very act of taking them, black people will achieve personal dignity, self-respect, and pride in color. It is to this end that The Woodlawn Organization came into being.

The basis for The Woodlawn Organization was people united for their own self-interest—a strong, politically independent community organization which would concern itself with the self-interest of people, to develop the kind of political sophistication that would bring to these people the power to make basic and fundamental changes in their lives here in their own neighborhood.

Many intelligent persons in the Woodlawn community possessed the capacity for leadership—Ollie Clark, Rosa Scott, James Grammer, Phyllis Hubbard, Lawrence Carroll, to name only a few. Before The Woodlawn Organization existed these persons would never have been considered leaders by City Hall or the downtown interests. But today they are a force to be reckoned with. These persons and others like them had a growing awareness of the need to organize, and an understanding that if organization was to be effective, outside resources were necessary. All knew that a great deal of money would be necessary to organize effectively because of the pervasive, historically rooted feeling of powerlessness in the black ghetto.

The leaders knew that the people they planned to organize were people whose individual relationships with those in authority had resulted in humiliation and defeat, from encounters with landlords, police, and school officials. The will of others was imposed upon the people in all of these situations. The leaders saw that the black man in Woodlawn, like the black man of the old South and of present Northern ghettos, was being politically exploited for the self-interest of others.

There are two sources of power in the body politic of this country: money and people. The ghetto has no money; but it has people, and people are more important than money. So in the ghetto there is power, raw power—plenty of people. Unorganized power, however, goes nowhere. This is not to imply that there has been no organization in the black ghetto. It has come, however, from the outside for the self-interest of others rather than for the self-interest of black people. A community with people organized from within provides the route from powerlessness to power. This route was followed by The Woodlawn Organization.

Chapter Two

TWO: A Response to Human Need

Woodlawn distrusted and feared white society. The fear of the white suburban man for the black ghetto cannot compare with the fear the ghetto dweller has for the white suburbs. The exploited and fearful people of Woodlawn did not appear on the surface to have the kind of stuff it takes to do such things as forcing the University of Chicago to come to terms with them on urban renewal, grappling with Mayor Daley on issues ranging from intolerable housing to inadequate schools, standing off the police, cleaning up unscrupulous business practices of some of Woodlawn's merchants, negotiating a million-dollar youth training program with the Office of Economic Opportunity, working with its own "gangs" in sponsoring and operating the program, and participating as an equal partner with the public schools of Chicago and the University of Chicago on an experimental school district.

Precisely these things happened on the south side of Chicago in the decade of the sixties. They came about through organization—The Woodlawn Organization. They happened because people in Woodlawn developed a near obsession for self-determination. They came about because the church cared and risked its reputation to step out and initiate action. They happened because some liberal subsystems of the establishment supported what was happening in Woodlawn. The Woodlawn Organization was not without its failures—failures that hurt but did not crush the organization.

How did all this come about? We look back a decade to where it started.

Four pastors in the community were deeply concerned about the conditions of Woodlawn in the late fifties.[1] Their many conversations continually came back to a basic inescapable conclusion that within two or three years Woodlawn would become a major slum unless a vigorous community organization was developed to stem the deterioration that was spreading across the community. Sensing that they would need help from the outside they agreed together that each would take the initiative in conferring with leaders of their respective church organizations for this help.

Church Leadership

At the request of the four pastors the national leaders of the churches to which they belonged met early in 1959 to consider the pastors' analysis of the desperate situation in Woodlawn. The pastors presented as an imperative that the national organizations of the churches support the efforts of the local congregations in organizing the community. The church leaders agreed that continued conversation and planning should be undertaken. The four pastors in the community drew up a document outlining the basic needs of the community as a first step.

The leaders took a second important step. The members of the Roman Catholic Church suggested that the Woodlawn community needed a powerful, hard-hitting community organizing program similar to that accomplished some years previously in the formation of the Back-of-the-Yards Council, by the Industrial Areas Foundation. The IAF, a controversial organization headed by Saul Alinsky, provides technical services to communities who want to organize themselves. This suggestion was taken seriously, and after a great deal of controversy the community turned to IAF for help.

As a third step the representatives of the Catholic Church offered to secure a $50,000 grant from Catholic sources to start such an organizational program if the Presbyterians and Lutherans would each contribute a similar amount. This financing, supple-

[1]They were Dr. Charles Leber and Dr. Ulysses Blakely, co-pastors of the First Presbyterian Church of Chicago; Father Martin Farrell, pastor of the Holy Cross Roman Catholic Church; Rev. Kenneth Profrock, pastor of the Woodlawn Emanuel Lutheran Church. Rev. Profrock later withdrew his support.

mented by available foundation grants, would provide a sufficient basis for the first three years of work. Representatives of the churches felt that at the end of three years the residents and institutions of the community would be fully ready to finance the lower cost of continuing a community-wide organization.

In April 1959, upon the recommendation of the church leaders the four pastors from Woodlawn drew up a document entitled *The Woodlawn Cooperative Project*, in which they stated:

> For more than a year the pastors of the Holy Cross Catholic Church, The Woodlawn Emanuel Lutheran Church, and the First Presbyterian Church of Chicago consulted with each other in regard to the tragic problems of social and physical deterioration of the Woodlawn community. In the process of attending meetings of various community and civic organizations, by participating in the activity and programs of these Woodlawn groups, by conversing with residents and block clubs, and by consulting widely with officials of other governmental, educational and religious organizations related to Woodlawn, these pastors found that 1) the Woodlawn community as a whole was not represented by any one organization; 2) that blight, over-crowding of residential buildings, transiency, crime and social disorganization was dangerously on the increase; 3) that this community deterioration began slowly during the depression of the thirties and was sharply accelerated by the housing shortage during World War II and was intensified by postwar inflation coupled with rent control; 4) that racial change in the community began around 1949 and 1950 and within six years the population became some 90 percent non-white. The first Negro residents were well-to-do, stable families seeking relief from the intolerable housing and social conditions of the ghetto further north and west. The same exploitive forces which plagued the Negro residents in Chicago for many years again capitalized on the racial change in the Woodlawn community in the following ways.
>
> A) Property acquisition through scare tactics, and panic selling.
>
> B) Conversion of larger apartments into smaller, cheaper quarters for a more transient and socially unstable population.
>
> C) Development of furnished kitchenette units in apartment hotels catering to all kinds of temporary and irresponsible occupants.
>
> D) Increase in tavern activity coupled with the influx of dope peddlers, prostitutes, and gambling interests.

The document went on to say that those who had sought to give leadership to the community had continually been divided against one another in a variety of personality, policy and organizational conflicts. Even the Woodlawn Ministers' Alliance had become inactive because of the division of loyalty among various community action groups and the general discouragement with the chaotic leadership pattern in the area. This document established firmly the need for the churches to become actively involved in improving the quality of living in the Woodlawn community.

The documented view of Woodlawn formulated by the four pastors was clearly supported by IAF director Saul Alinsky, who stated in a letter to Dr. Charles Leber:

> Woodlawn is typical of a great many communities in our major urban centers, communities which have become known as the inner-city, communities which were previously all white and have as a result of the population movements of the past decade, become all Negro, communities which present many color problems not only to the local residents but to the larger city about them, communities possessed of major institutions such as churches which had been normally attended by the previous residents which are now faced with a whole new population, communities which are hot with change, communities boiling with mobility and daily deterioration into worse and worse slums, communities which have no control force with which to cope with any of the problems from without or within. The organizations of the previous citizens fled their area with their people and the new people did not have the roots or ties to the community to be concerned. And so there is no organization of the new. . . . Local residents have only one desire and that is to secure the economic means with which to move out.

A successful community organization in Woodlawn would be the first demonstration that the resources in this kind of community can be used effectively to bring about major benefits not only to those particular communities but to the city surrounding these areas as well.

IAF Leadership

How was it that the leaders of the Woodlawn community enlisted the aid of the Industrial Areas Foundation in self-organization? Why did they not go to some other group to seek out help? The fundamental philosophy of IAF was wholly acceptable to the people and leaders of Woodlawn. The IAF did not insist upon giving direction to the organization although they brought in staff members from outside the community. If IAF had given direction to the organization it would have failed in its organizing efforts in Woodlawn. The people would have seen this to be the same kind of paternalism they were trying to throw off. Even though in the early stages of The Woodlawn Organization the staff was being paid by the IAF, it was clearly understood that the staff was to carry out the policy set down by the delegate assembly of the Woodlawn Organization.

The staff took a role of counselling, advising, and actually carrying out the policies of the organization, but the staff never took a leadership role, nor did they make reports to the steering committee or to the house of delegates. At no time was an IAF staff man in control of the organization.

The philosophy of the IAF was clearly spelled out in a letter written by Saul Alinsky to Dr. Leber, who was at that time co-pastor of the First Presbyterian Church of Chicago.

> As to the issue of the basic philosophy of the Industrial Areas Foundation, it should be remembered that the Industrial Areas Foundation's tactics and principles must be dictated and formed by the specific society and community we are working in. At no time and in no place does the Industrial Areas Foundation enter into a situation with a preconceived idea of what is to be done or how it should be accomplished.
>
> Some of the most important reasons for our not having a carefully worked out pre-packaged approach to a given organizational undertaking is that all we do is contingent on the wishes of the people who are forming a new organization. The very pith and marrow of our work is the creating of a vehicle that permits the individual a greater say in the circumstances that govern his life.
>
> The Industrial Areas Foundation only exercises and controls to the extent of refusing to lend aid or encouragement to groups and individuals whose true purpose is contrary to the letter or spirit of the nation's laws. For instance; if we were working in a community that had an element in it that was anti-Negro, we would refuse to allow our talents to be used to suppress Negro rights more efficiently. By the same token we cannot cooperate with communists or gangsters. But omitting these dangerous extremes, our policy is to manage to find ways to get people and institutions to work in a community and when the policies of that organization are attacked as not being in accord with "moral

principles", the accusers should not look at us for an explanation or a defense. They should go to the churches, the businessmen, all the organized forces in the community in question because the policies under attack are theirs, not ours. We cannot be the keepers of other men's consciences. That does not mean we are indifferent to moral questions. Quite the contrary, that is why we believe every person and every institution must realize his own moral responsibilities and we trust that our work has frequently helped many to do exactly that.

Our job is to create situations in which people can think and act constructively and effectively on the serious moral problems which are theirs. We do firmly believe that when people have the opportunity, they will live up to the highest expectations.

In the last analysis, the people themselves decide on the tactics they use. Actually, we cannot organize a community. The community does it itself. The statement may be surprising but simple arithmetic bears it out. How can four or five men walk into a place where 50,000 people are living and organize them? They cannot! Essentially what they can do is get the people to organize themselves. As a simple matter of fact, it would take five men two years just to talk to everybody in a community of that size. No! It is not we who do the organizing. That is done by the people who are being organized and it is for that reason that they can be organized. We are never in the position of being an outside group rushing in to tell people what to do. They tell us what they are going to do and work out ways of doing it. We have as much and the same kind of relationship to organizational tactics as the mid-wife has to the birth of a baby. It is the community and above all its leaders, its ministers, its social and economic leaders who decide what the tactics are to be. It is their responsibility to do nothing they will ever be ashamed of having a part in.

IAF was acceptable to The Woodlawn Organization because its staff did not enter into negotiations with city agencies. This was done by the people of the community. The president of The Woodlawn Organization, committee chairmen and other designated people negotiated, made reports to the steering committee and delegate assembly and made statements to the public.

The offer of the Catholic Church to raise $50,000 to contribute to the Industrial Areas Foundations served as a pump-primer for other monies to come into The Woodlawn Organization. The Schwartzhaupt Foundation contributed $69,000 and $21,000 came from the First Presbyterian Church of Chicago. The Woodlawn Organization had enough money to begin operations.

An early internal controversy, however, threatened to disrupt the infant community organization. As soon as The Woodlawn Organization began to consider inviting the Industrial Areas Foundation into the community some members of the Woodlawn Ministers' Alliance began to question the wisdom and propriety of this move. The discussion was prolonged, heated and intense. A handful of Protestant pastors within the alliance, while showing concern for organizing the community, stood in opposition to inviting the Industrial Areas Foundation into the community. Those who opposed the IAF continued to allude to what they considered the immoral organizing tactics of Saul Alinsky, director of the IAF. When pressed to specify what these immoral tactics were, however, they were unable to give concrete examples.

Members of the alliance made a thorough study of the charges and in a written review of their findings made the following statement:

> Power itself is neither moral or immoral. The uses to which power is put are moral or immoral. A democratic society pursuing the path of free enterprise is based upon power concepts. The relationship of any institution or group to power cannot be avoided. All of society is involved in continual power struggles for supremacy. To refuse to be involved is to let yourself be used usually by the most cunning and unscrupulous. Assertions that IAF is dangerous because of its power principle of organization are sentimental. There is no organization that means anything at all that doesn't depend upon power for every facet of its existence as an organization, internally and externally.
>
> To say that IAF abuses power is a serious assertion. It is our firm conviction that this assertion is not capable of being validated. *Is Alinsky a tool of the Catholic Church?* What validates this charge? We have not yet seen the person or argument that can make the charges stick. Alinsky has aided many Roman Catholics to understand the principles of community organization. We are certain that they have made good use of this understanding. He has been willing and eager to teach the staff of the National Council of Churches the same principles. He is by conviction anti-authoritarian, equalitarian, humanistic. He is rabidly anti-sectarian. His services are sought by industry, unions, churches and civic organizations.

The research findings of the pastors ended the debate and the Woodlawn Ministers' Alliance invited the Industrial Areas Foundation into Woodlawn to begin its organizational activities.

The discussion within the alliance generated a development of singular importance. It began to be obvious that the Woodlawn Ministers' Alliance was purely a Protestant alliance. If the church as a whole was to play a meaningful role in the physical and social rehabilitation of the community, close cooperation between Protestant and Catholic churches in Woodlawn was absolutely essential. The dialogue with the Catholic pastors in the community got under way. The key figures in the dialogue were Father Farrell, Dr. Leber and Dr. Blakely. The dialogue centered around the name of the organization. As long as the word "Ministers" was used in the organization's title, the Catholic pastors felt that they could not participate. The Woodlawn Ministers' Alliance accordingly changed its name to the Greater Woodlawn Pastors' Alliance, forging into one alliance both the Catholic and the Protestant pastors who were destined to play a leading and dynamic role in forming The Woodlawn Organization.

It is significant that the religious leaders of Woodlawn and not the political or business leaders first saw the need for a strong organization in the community. Many people believe the pastor should limit his activities to Sunday morning sermons, counseling those of his parishioners who are having difficulties, and visiting the sick. The Greater Woodlawn Pastors' Alliance, however, felt that while ministers should continue to function in their traditional role they should not close their eyes to the very real suffering and human misery caused by the exploitative forces in the community. An early draft of the constitution and by-laws of the Greater Woodlawn Pastors' Alliance stated, "This Alliance is based upon the belief that a community's religious institutions can and must make a contribution to the general welfare of the people that transcends the ordinary concerns of the church."

So The Woodlawn Organization was born. Power was being generated and organized in the Woodlawn area. A people-oriented organization from its very inception, TWO had the support also of most of the churches in the community. It had the consulting service and staff provided by the Industrial Areas Foundation. The following chapters tell of the struggles, triumphs, and frustrations of The Woodlawn Organization.

Chapter Three

TWO: Organized Around Issues

One mistake novices at organizing a community make is to rush out and try to obtain dramatic victories at the very outset. More often than not they fail. The overzealous organizer who does not really understand what his role should be will pick an issue that is very important to the people so he can organize everyone around that one issue. So important an issue, however, is often too difficult for the community to win in the beginning stages of organization. The people do not have the necessary power. When they lose their first battle the organization begins to deteriorate.

Residents of ghettos are exceedingly skeptical about community organizations. They feel, "Well, we've been in organizations before; we've heard this kind of talk before; we have fought and nothing has come of it, so why should we do it over again? We will wait and see if this organization can do anything before we become involved." It is important to win a first battle.

The Woodlawn Organization organized around many issues—issues that affected as many people as possible. If TWO had taken only one issue, only the people interested in that issue would have become involved. The first action, then, was to get out into the community, talk with people, listen to them, find out what kinds of things they were angry about or concerned about.

Priorities must be set up in a fledgling community organization. Taking action on every idea that comes to the attention of the organization is ineffective. Selection is of prime importance. The criterion for action is not necessarily that the issue be the largest one or even the most important one. The issue must be one that the organization can win—an issue that will solidify the organization and demonstrate its power in a small but significant way. This is what TWO did, as we shall see, when it marched in protest against unscrupulous merchants who were bilking the Woodlawn residents.

Indigenous Leadership

Not only must the community organization deal with problems that are of concern to all the people, it must also draw upon indigenous leadership. Indigenous leadership is imperative because the black man must learn that he does not have to rely upon leadership that the white power structure appoints for him. When this happens, as it has in the past, whites invariably take over. Black organizations need their own leaders. Whether the whites like it or not they must begin to live with the black leaders that the black people themselves appoint, just as black people have had to learn to live with the Theodore Bilbo, the James Eastlands, and the George Wallaces.

The organization has to provide a way whereby the indigenous leaders are identified. Just asking community people, "I wonder who is a leader here," is not responsible planning. People must have an opportunity to act and to do things, to participate over a period of time. Leadership cannot be appointed from the top. The people reject that kind of leadership just as they reject downtown leadership.

Working committees and subcommittees and informal groups must be set up to attract a large number of participants. As they work on these committees, persons who are interested in doing more work have an opportunity to do so. When the committee structure is open-ended so that those who are interested can move up in the organizational structure, there is a route for indigenous leaders to take on more and more responsibility.

The Woodlawn Organization needed a president and a staff director. The president would be an indigenous person, elected by the total membership of TWO. He would not be paid as president, for otherwise seeds of disruption would be sown, in that the office would then become a political one, and all kinds of political activity would surround the office.

The Formal Structure of TWO

In the early days TWO stood for Temporary Woodlawn Organization. Later the name became The Woodlawn Organization and kept the same initials, TWO.

The purposes of TWO gradually clarified as work began. Formally speaking, TWO is an organization of civic, religious, business, and other community groups that have pledged themselves in a cooperative venture to work together for the improvement and the enrichment of life in modern urban society. This organization was brought into being over a period of time for the preservation of the community strength, for the maintenance of community power to deal effectively and efficiently with problems that upset wholesome community living. TWO's basic aim is to work for a well-ordered society wherein there is a sincere concern for the general welfare of all the people, without regard to race, color, religious creed, national origin, or social station. TWO strives for social justice in the areas of housing, education, health, employment, and government.

TWO is pledged to take the initiative in developing adequate standards and values for community living. The dynamics of urban society call for attentiveness and action if the community is to keep healthfully alive. TWO intends to pursue this course unrelentingly.

Individuals as such do not and cannot belong to TWO as voting members. Voting membership is by organization. Any organization in Woodlawn which is, at least in part, civic in objective, and which approves of and is willing to abide by and actively support the aims of TWO, may become a member upon application. The application must be approved by a majority of the members of the delegates meeting. Individuals may become sponsoring members, but they may not participate actively in the organization nor possess voting privileges.

Member organizations do not lose their individual identity, but remain sovereign with respect to their own business and affairs. Member organizations pay dues of a minimum of $125 a year. Larger groups and organizations contribute more.

Every member group selects five delegates and two alternates to represent it at the *delegates meeting.* The delegates meet at least once a month to conduct the ordinary business of the organization, to hear committee reports from the standing committees and other committees, to review the interim decisions of the steering committee, to dispense money, and to implement the policies of the annual convention. The delegate committee has the final authority on all matters of policy implementation.

TWO holds an annual convention each year on or before May 31. The *annual convention* is composed of all member organizations who are current on their dues, fifty dollars of which must be paid as a convention fee. Such organizations are entitled to send seven delegates and five alternates to the convention. The annual convention has the power to create standing committees, to amend the constitution, to elect all officers including the chairman of the annual convention, and to pass resolutions laying down the mandatory policies of the organization for the coming year. No officer of the organization may serve as a chairman of the annual convention. A special convention may be called upon request of 60 percent of the member organizations and sponsoring members.

The officers of the organization are the president, executive vice-president, vice-president, secretary, treasurer, corresponding secretary, assistant treasurer, and sergeant-at-arms.

Besides the house of delegates, TWO has another representative body, the *steering committee,* designed to carry out the organizational functions. It is comprised of the president and all the vice-presidents, all elected officers, and the standing-committee chairmen. The steering committee functions as an executive committee, and is responsible to the house of delegates. The steering committee hears all the standing-committee reports, keeps the organization functioning effectively, and acts as supervisory committee to the president.

The *housing committee* hears all complaints from residents of the community concerning code violations, follows through on these and makes its own inspection where possible. On valid complaints the committee contacts the owner or his agent and asks to have the matter corrected. The housing committee moves as fast as possible on all complaints, because it is important that the people of the community know there is an organization to which they can carry their complaints and get results.

The *schools committee* concentrates on ways of getting better education for the children in the community. It works with PTA's where possible; but if the local PTA group is found to be no more than an arm of the principal and not willing to tackle the basic issues concerning education in the ghetto, the committee sets out to form a local Parents Education Council. The schools committee is concerned with all the problems of the schools and works with them.

The *community maintenance committee* hears any complaints concerning failure of the city to remove garbage or sweep the streets or remove snow when necessary. It also surveys the community from time to time to make observations on its own.

The *consumer practices committee* hears and investigates all complaints concerning unscrupulous business practices. If the businessman is guilty the committee seeks redress for the complainant. The committee recognizes that much more work needs to be done in this area than adjudicating individual complaints, and tries to find ways to deal with the problem of unscrupulous business practices at several levels.

The *social welfare committee* works closely with the residents who receive some form of public assistance. The committee finds that much of its work is in providing information for recipients regarding the benefits to which they are entitled, and in helping secure these benefits. This committee has been so helpful to clients that one state legislator accused TWO of being one of the organizations responsible for an increase in aid to recipients.

The *civil rights committee* hears and investigates all complaints that come to it from persons who feel they have in some way been deprived of their civil rights. This has led the committee to investigate many cases of alleged police brutality. The committee has also received and investigated complaints for persons who have not been able to get proper emergency treatment, either because of discriminatory practices or lack of cash money.

The *fund-raising committee* has the responsibility of raising funds for the organization. The annual banquet is the culmination of the year's fund-raising activities.

Organizations such as TWO must be established throughout the city of Chicago and in other cities of the country. A network of related organizations across the country will assure the black man of a real place in the main currents of American life.

Chapter Four

Early Struggles of TWO

Woodlawn had taken the plunge. This was to be no ordinary civil rights movement, but an organized structure based on the self-determining powers of the people, and coming into confrontation with the existing power structure. Conflict would grow, and controversy would multiply. TWO sensed this only vaguely at the time, but the organization was preparing for the extensive conflict that did indeed develop.

The chief organizer for the Industrial Areas Foundation early in 1961 was Nicholas Von Hoffman, now an author and feature writer for the *Washington Post*.[1] He took up his position in the community along with his staff, Robert Squires, Edgar Jamison, Richard Harmon, and Jeff Williams. With the help of community leaders he planned an initial organizational meeting designed to attract as many groups in Woodlawn as possible to become members of the yet-to-be formed Woodlawn Organization. Such groups as Woodlawn Block Club Council, the Woodlawn Businessmen's Association, the Greater Woodlawn Pastors' Alliance, and the United Woodlawn Conference were represented at the initial meeting.[2] Individuals could join only by being members of groups that would represent them.

---

[1]Two of Von Hoffman's books are *Mississippi Notebook* and *We Are The People Our Parents Warned Us About.*

[2]The United Woodlawn Conference felt that its own position in the community was being threatened by the formation of this new organization. This group felt that the interests of all the groups and the community at large would not be better served by coming together under one umbrella organization, but that they should work out community problems as individual organizations. The United Woodlawn Conference walked out of the initial meeting and was never a part of TWO. The UWC went into a sharp decline and soon went out of existence.

The new group first chose a name, Temporary Woodlawn Organization. This indicated that the organizational structure was of a temporary nature, to ensure that all new groups who would later come into the organization would have a determining voice in drafting the final constitution and in selecting the organization's permanent officers.

The group established temporary by-laws and elected a temporary president, Rev. Robert J. McGee, assistant pastor of the Apostolic Church of God. They designated Rev. Arthur M. Brazier to be the official spokesman for TWO. After that meeting organizing activities began in earnest. Almost immediately new organizations began to join TWO. Among them were the Future Outlook League and several Puerto Rican organizations.

A fundamental principle of TWO from its founding has been that the people of Woodlawn themselves, not some outside agency, would determine what their problems were. This is a radical democratic principle, one that runs counter to the operation of almost every political, social, and educational institution in the land that has to do with the ghetto. It cuts across white paternalism, "colonial welfarism," and educational do-goodism, all of which are based on the operating principle that those higher up are superior and know best, their high-sounding proclamations about democratic principles notwithstanding. Such institutions may permit acquiescence, but nothing more. When the people themselves define their problems, however, the status quo is threatened and the Establishment moves in quickly to defend its position.

Pinpointing the Problems

The role of the IAF staff members at this time was to uncover the real concerns of the residents of Woodlawn. To do this they went to the people where they were, talked with them, and watched what was going on. This procedure led them to street corners, bars, homes, churches—wherever the people of Woodlawn lived their lives.

A number of complaints began to be articulated. The grievance that stood out above all others was the exploitation, lying, and cheating by some of the businessmen in the area. Credit buying was enslaving some of the residents of Woodlawn. Overcharging, a common practice in most slum areas, was rampant. Woodlawnites were found to be victims of underweighing, of shoddy merchandise, of false cash register totals. A number of the groups joined TWO at this time with the expressed concern of doing something about such unscrupulous practices.

Not all the businessmen of the area were guilty of these unfair practices. The Woodlawn Businessmen's Association was one of the first groups to become a member of TWO. Through the leadership and vision of businessmen such as George Kyros, Morris Kaplan, and Ben Cowell, all of whom were leading merchants in the community, the Woodlawn Businessmen's Association became a charter member of TWO. The Association worked with TWO to expose those businessmen who were taking unfair advantage of the consumer in the community. They felt that unfair business was doing a great deal of harm to business as well as customer interests.

Attacking Unfair Business Practices

Here was an issue made to order for a vigorous young organization ready to flex its muscles. TWO's action illustrates several important principles of community organization. To act on this issue would serve the needs of many people; it was a dramatic, indigenous issue; it was relatively small; it was a battle that TWO could probably win; results would come quickly; it promised to give TWO a great deal of publicity; it was an issue on which TWO and honest businessmen could unite. For TWO to take on a major problem involving a long fight with a powerful organization that might have been victorious over TWO would have been disastrous. A first defeat is the last one for a newly formed community. First a skirmish that could be won, later the war of confrontation—that was the order of the day.

TWO wanted to expose unscrupulous businessmen and confront them with an angry, determined community. What was the most effective tactic? TWO organized a gigantic Square Deal Parade down 63rd Street, the main business section of Woodlawn. Since this demonstration was to be the organization's first tactic, leaders cautioned all of the people about the need for orderly procedure and nonviolence. TWO notified the police department of the parade and pointed out to them that it would be a peaceful demonstration. The committee found it difficult to secure a parade permit, but the local ward committeeman worked closely with TWO, and with his help the parade permit was issued. The Square Deal Parade was carried out as scheduled. More than a thousand singing, sign-carrying citizens gave effective vent to their years of frustration over exploitation by unscrupulous white merchants. The parade was a resounding success. It made headlines in all major Chicago newspapers.

But TWO went beyond headlines. The effect of the heady wine of a successful demonstration quickly wanes, and the threat to local unscrupulous businessmen would have faded as people lost interest. The demonstration itself brought about no real changes. The situation called for follow-up exposure and confrontation. The following week TWO set up a check-out counter in the yard of a Catholic church near the business district. The people of Woodlawn who suspected they had just been cheated checked the accuracy of the weights of goods they had purchased from stores in the area on the registered scale. A scoreboard recorded the results. TWO then distributed leaflets throughout the community naming offending merchants and urging citizens of the area to boycott them.

Another tactic was created. TWO invited people to bring purchases they suspected of being shoddy or falsely advertised, such as radios that did not play, or used clothing sold as new, to public meetings. Each person told his story in front of the whole assembly. TWO, through its committee, took the case in hand, studied the claims of the persons, and if their complaint was legitimate, took it up with the merchants. The offended party, when given redress, once more appeared before the TWO meeting, told of the restitution that had been made, and thanked both TWO and the merchant for the square deal received. Each instance was another small but meaningful victory for the people.

Behind this public activity stood solid organizational work by TWO and its staff. In cooperation with the Businessmen's Association, TWO and some of the ministers and indigenous leaders who were beginning to step forward drew up a Code of Business Ethics covering credit practices, pricing, and advertising. To make the code stick, TWO established a board of arbitration consisting of four businessmen from the Businessmen's Association, four community people representing consumer groups, and an impartial chairman from outside Woodlawn, chosen by the board.

TWO won the battle. Dishonest business practices sharply declined. TWO's prestige soared, and new groups joined the organization. TWO was ready to take on some tougher issues. But some internal problems took priority at this time.

Five members of the Woodlawn Pastors' Alliance, a group that had a membership in TWO, raised questions about the morality of the street demonstration and the tactics of applying pressure to the businessmen in the community. Their major arguments centered about the use of power to attain ends that were in the best interest of the poor people in the area. Their arguments were in essence the same they had raised earlier in the debate over engaging the services of Saul Alinsky and the IAF.

They spoke against the peaceful demonstration by the citizens of the community on the grounds that it was immoral. Other members of the alliance felt they should instead have spoken against the kind of business practices that were wreaking havoc with the finances of the poorest segment of the community on the grounds that *this* was immoral. The majority agreed that the real questions of morality had to do with the way some businessmen were making judgments against the poor people; the way they were constantly guilty of misleading advertising; how they sold shoddy merchandise at inflated prices; how they charged exorbitant interest rates and carrying charges; how merchants refused to give all legal documents to the customers when final payment had been made.

When four of these ministers, three white and one Negro, were forbidden to use a tape recorder at the alliance meetings and when it became clear that their point of view would never prevail, they withdrew from the Greater Woodlawn Pastors' Alliance. They formed their own alliance, which has never become really involved in the everyday life of the people of the community.

Their withdrawal, however, made headlines in one of the city newspapers, crowding to the second page such sensational news as the orbiting of Russia's first manned spacecraft. In response to the newspaper publicity, Dr. Ulysses Blakely, co-pastor of the First Presbyterian Church of Chicago and president of the Greater Woodlawn Pastors' Alliance, issued the following statement:

> We regret the decision of the four churches to withdraw from our Alliance. Needless to say, the majority of Woodlawn churches will continue to work together for the physical and social rehabilitation of our community. The Greater Woodlawn Pastors' Alliance is an unusual organization composed of a broad spectrum of religious beliefs, ranging from Pentecostal to Roman Catholic to Presbyterian. There is no other Alliance like it and we are deeply sorry that our four departed brethren no longer wish to share our fellowship in it. The news of their resignation does not come as a surprise to us. Three of the members have resigned previously only to change their minds and return to our group. If they decide to come back another time, they know we will again extend a hand of Christian fellowship. Their leaving will not affect the work being done in the community nor the community's unity, in as much as they represent various small, struggling churches which remain here by virtue of outside monetary subsidies. Subsidized institutions like these are very susceptible to outside pressure. We believe this explains why the four subsidized institutions have acted as they have. We were offered a chance to have the splinter group stay with us. That price is too high in our opinion. We elected to stick with the people and work on behalf of the people's program. The four churches have taken another road. We think that this is a tragic mistake. In the long-run, the churches of our community must serve the people in our community and stand with them.*

While this was going on inside the Greater Woodlawn Pastors' Alliance, TWO continued its organizing activities, bringing into the organization new community groups and strengthening its organizational structure.

Rent Strikes

In 1961 and 1962, TWO was searching for a method to deal effectively with the slum landlord. Most slum lords were absentee owners who hid behind land trusts. These trusts were held by banks who refused to divulge the names of the true owners. Even when TWO did eventually locate them it was almost impossible to get the trusts or the owners to make meaningful repairs on their property. Many of the slum buildings were infested with rats and vermin because no regular exterminator services were maintained.

---

*All four ministers have since given up their pastorates in the community.

In many cases the plumbing was in an abominable state of disrepair, and electrical violations were rampant. TWO found that most of the absentee owners were oblivious to pleas for repairs. TWO then decided that the only way to force the slumlord to listen was to strike him where it hurt most—in the pocketbook.

TWO conducted the first rent strike in the nation. When a rent strike—the withholding of rent money until certain repairs are made—was first proposed, there were strident cries that this was an immoral action. The people who spoke against rent strikes offered no solution other than the same old ineffective approach of taking the owner into court. In many cases where this was done, the owner would get a small fine. The complaining tenant would be evicted by an indignant and revengeful landlord who would then rent to another tenant and carry on his "business as usual" operation.

Despite criticism, however, TWO began to organize entire buildings for strikes. The tenants who were being victimized readily cooperated with an organization concerned with their plight.

Big slum operators are doing millions of dollars of business in slum property. It is pure folly to attack a big slum operator and call a rent strike on him. He can absorb a rent strike on a six-flat building, for example, because he is making so much money on other property. A better tactic is to go after the less affluent slum owner, the man who has purchased buildings and wants to make an investment and get as much money out of it as he can, not caring what happens to the building. The small owner who has bought a bad building that does not provide enough income for repairs is a separate problem. Sometimes the city can be persuaded to buy the building and repair it.

The real slum operator, however—one who does not keep his building up but is small enough to need the money from it—is the right target. Here is an example: a six-flat in *x* block. The building was not properly heated; the janitor did not carry out the garbage; the floors in the hallway were not swept; the plaster was falling; the windows sagged. The TWO committee went to the slum landlord to try to negotiate with him. He refused to listen, and ordered the committee out of his office. His whole history of dealing with black people conditioned him to treat them that way. The committee asked him to come to TWO with his lawyer and negotiate, but he failed to appear. The time had come to strike.

TWO collected the evidence, taking pictures of fallen plaster, exposed wiring, filthy toilets that would not flush, sagging windows stuffed with rags. TWO then said to the people, "No one pays rent. Everybody must stick together. We will go to court with you because the landlord will try to put you out. The landlord will go after one to put fear into everyone else. He will try to find the weakest person. But you have to make up your minds that in order to have a decent place to live you have to work together. No one is going to come in and do it for you. We cannot fight your battles for you, but we will fight them with you if you are willing to help yourselves."

The rent money was held in escrow and not spent. TWO then put signs saying RENT STRIKE in the inside of the windows for all to see. In the windows of another apartment a sign read THIS IS A SLUM BUILDING. TWO called television stations and suggested they take pictures of this terrible building. This upset the landlord, of course. His name was in the newspapers and on television. On one occasion a landlord rushed into an apartment and snatched one of the signs out of the window. He was arrested for destroying private property.

When TWO brought the landlord to court three or four hundred persons crowded into the courtroom. When the case was called, all of them went up to the court bench with the complainant to support him. The lawyer showed the judge the pictures of the conditions. (At no point has a judge said that a rent strike is legal, but because of the interest and the evidence, the judge does take time to study the matter.) The lawyer for the landlord was frantic when the judge continued the case. The people were still in the building and no rent was being paid, so he came in and negotiated. We had about $3000 of his money, and we gave it to him, but first he signed an agreement to do a number of things to repair the property. TWO intimated that if repairs were not made they would conduct another rent strike.

A rent strike against a big landlord involves different tactics. The people must withhold their rent for about six weeks without getting nervous and defecting one by one. The big landlord can afford to lose money for four or five weeks, so a quick settlement must be effected.

TWO picketed big slumlords at their suburban homes. There is now a law on the books making it possible to locate building owners, but when TWO was first organized the owner was difficult to locate, because the buildings were held in trust. The TWO committee would go to the bank and ask the name of the building owner. When the bankers would not divulge that information the committee promised that a delegation would visit the bank president the next Saturday. The committee would consider the bank as owner of the property, because the bank was collecting the rents through an agent.

The hundred-man delegation would visit the bank, not to picket, but just to stand around. In view of the bad image this gave the bank—all those black people hanging around—the bank would drop the trust and reveal the owner's name. Then TWO would picket him at his home. His place of business was usually in a black neighborhood and that would not hurt him. But it put real pressure on him when his neighbors found he was making money in this immoral way. Court procedure followed, with TWO asking the court to take the building into receivership.

In the final analysis, however, the rent strike is not the answer to deplorable housing in the ghetto. The rent strike can dramatize the issue. It can bring relief to a few people, but it does not and cannot deal effectively with it because of the immensity of the problem. The real pressure must be put on the city, because it has the power to deal effectively with the situation.

School Problems

The school creates a different problem from that of the slum landlord or the unscrupulous merchant. It is something that one local community organization finds very difficult to deal with, for it is a city-wide operation. The local community must deal with it locally, however, because one way to make a community a desirable place to live in is to offer good education in the local schools. So the community organization cannot escape the problem because of its city-wide nature. TWO had to begin to deal with it.

It should be made very clear from the outset that ghetto schools are abysmal failures. School people have often declared the slum child uneducable, and they have thrown their failures on the backs of the parents. They point out that the children come from underprivileged homes where there are no books. It is obvious that American education is going to fail if the whole educational system is designed to meet the needs of the white middle-class child, who comes out of an environment where there are books and educated parents, where even the language spoken is significantly different from that of the slum child. If the educational system is designed to that level hundreds of thousands of children who come from different backgrounds are not going to become educated. Our educational system must devise some new approaches to education, just as education devised new approaches to teaching the hard of hearing and the blind. Educators must meet the needs, not just shed tears about the underprivileged homes. When these children grow up with no real education to help them function in our present-day society, they become a public charge. The schools have become islands in the community, especially in Chicago. They have become a four-walled fortress, the scene of failure for hundreds of thousands of youngsters.

At one time the schools in Chicago were so defensive that a citizen could not pick up a telephone and call a school directly. He had to call downtown to the Board of Education, and someone at the board office decided whether or not to put the call through. The schools still discourage visitors. A citizen can come only at a certain time, perhaps between 8:30 and 9:00 in the morning, on the grounds that this prevents any disruption of the class.

The curriculum is foreign to ghetto life. The middle-class first readers—"See the cow. See the beautiful grass."—are not oriented toward reality for the ghetto children. Such a child finds it very hard to relate to Dick and Jane in a small town with beautiful lawns, tricycles, and the friendly corner policeman. In fact, Dick and Jane, representing white society, are a threat to the very survival of black children. Even new readers are only slightly better. Although they feature urban life and black as well as white characters, they still fail to reach ghetto children.

One problem in the early days was the overcrowding of schools. Practically all Woodlawn children were on the double shift. The entire black community of Chicago accepted the double shift because they were not aware that 80 percent of the children in Chicago on the double shift were black children. They thought this was the condition all over the city, but it was not. There were three hundred empty classrooms in other parts of the city. This knowledge impelled The Woodlawn Organization to charge the Board of Education with segregation. Other groups, like the NAACP and the Urban League, had addressed themselves to that issue in speeches and statements made before the Board of Education. The Woodlawn Organization provided the impetus for public attack. TWO picketed the Board of Education and brought out into the open by public demonstration that the board was, in fact, segregating black children.

It was not a formal charge; no suit was filed. It was a *public* charge, however, that the Board of Education was, like the Board of Education in Alabama, practicing segregation.

This charge was published in the public media. The board denied this charge, of course. They indicated that the only reason there were all-black schools was that Chicago has the neighborhood system. The argument of TWO was that the Board of Education is charged with the responsibility of educating the children. If there is one school district that is too crowded to permit effective teaching of the children, and another school district that has empty classrooms, it is the board's responsibility to transport children from that overcrowded district to the empty classrooms, so that education can proceed. The board would not do this. The Board of Education was in an indefensible position.

Then the board did finally act. It devised a method of getting the black children off the double shift, yet keeping them in the black neighborhoods. They did that by buying millions of dollars worth of mobile classrooms, which TWO named "Willis Wagons," the Superintendent at that time being Benjamin C. Willis. They bought "Willis Wagons"; they purchased old ramshackle buildings; they purchased warehouses and remodeled them into classrooms. They claimed that as a great victory; but they very effectively kept the blacks in the ghetto.

Although TWO realized this was a city-wide problem, it was important to fight as a community organization, because the schools in this district were poor. To highlight the problem TWO called a school strike on the Carnegie School. That school strike was 90 percent effective.

The strike was held only one day. A school strike cannot be carried on for a long period of time. First of all there are many parents who work. There is nothing for their children to do. Parents do not want these youngsters on the streets. So a school strike begins to dissipate after the third or fourth day.

There were newspaper editorials stating, "A day out of class is a day out of the life of a child's education," and "The children in the ghetto need education badly and the misguided leaders in the ghetto are preventing the children from getting this education. Any education is better than no education at all." An editor's visit to a ghetto school might have made him question that last statement.

Black parents in the ghetto must understand that their children are getting an abysmal education; that they are not prepared to compete equally in our society; and that we are just fooling these children when we tell them to stay until they receive their diploma and all will be well. We must do something about these poor conditions. We must change the quality of education in the schools. Chapter Six will discuss some ways TWO sought to do this.

When young people receive their high school diploma many of them are functioning only on the 9th or 10th-grade level. The dropout rate in the state colleges of black students who graduated from segregated high schools is shameful, because the young people cannot do college work. As for passing college entrance exams for private colleges, this is almost an impossibility for the ghetto student. A few do pass in spite of poor segregated high school education, but very few.

It would seem that whatever their intrinsic merits, all the compensatory programs such as Upward Bound and Head Start are failures in that they are not changing the educational system itself. As soon as a child is out of that temporary phase of compensatory education and back in the system, he loses within a year or two whatever he has gained.

Meaningful experimentation must go on in the school system. This experimentation can involve the whole community. The organized community should have some voice in choosing the principal in that school. Right now the community has nothing to say about the choice of a principal. A man may be well qualified academically and administratively to run a middle-class white school. His psychological point of view toward black children and the black community may make him unqualified in the ghetto. A principal who thinks that black children are animals cannot educate them.

The community need not select teachers, but the community should have some input. The community organization should know who their principal will be. The organization should be able to discuss with their principal their views toward black children and their education. The community ought to be able to say to the district administration, "That principal is not the kind we want in our school. We are not passing on his academic qualifications; we are concerned about his attitude toward black children and ghetto schools. We think that psychologically this person does not fit this particular school." Admittedly, finding the right person is no easy task; but the administration must take cognizance of the community's expectation.

At this point in time no one in the community has any voice in the matter. A principal who has been put in stays in, even if he is totally unacceptable. In a white middle-class community, pressure can be brought to bear and a principal removed. This is no judgment against the white community. It is a judgment against the black community for not insisting that their alderman accompany them to the superintendent's office to protest and to ask for a better principal.

This is in part a political problem. Members of the black community have in the past blindly voted for an alderman on the sole ground that he was a Democrat. Even a black alderman, however, has often not been responsive to the people who elected him, because he was dependent upon the patronage system, not on the black community. At this time the white political structure still controls the patronage system, so the black alderman is responsive to the white political structure rather than to the black community.

When people of color vote for the man who will articulate their interests, instead of blindly voting a party line, changes can be made. An alderman working with his people can bring pressure to bear, and such a problem as removal of a poor principal will then be made possible.

Chapter Five

Battle with Urban Renewal

Just when TWO was beginning to flex its muscles, it was confronted by a giant that struck fear, hostility, and despair into the hearts of the people. The giant was the University of Chicago. Its weapon of destruction was a plan for urban renewal in Woodlawn.

The news of the university's plan for urban renewal first broke on the Woodlawn community in an article by Ruth Moore in the *Chicago Sun Times* dated July 20, 1960. It stated:

> A 75 million dollar enlargement of the University of Chicago's south of the Midway campus plus the clearing of the slums that surround it was proposed today. Chancellor Lawrence A. Kimpton and University Trustees made the proposal under a new federal law that would bring the city of Chicago not only the six million 500 thousand dollars needed for the clearance of the area, but an estimated wind-fall of 14 million 400 thousand dollars in federal urban renewal funds. The 14 million 400 thousand dollars could be used for any other urban renewal or conservation project in any part of the city and would be available to Chicago without the city having to contribute even a cent of its own funds. The University officials said under the new law the University expenditures in an urban renewal area (the University is in the Hyde Park-Kenwood area) can be counted as the required one-third local contribution to urban renewal. . . . The city would obtain 14 million 400 thousand dollars clear without being required to provide one cent of matching funds. The proposal was laid before the Chicago land clearance commission at its meeting at 320 North Clark. The University asked the Commission to declare the south campus area as urban

renewal project and to undertake an immediate survey to qualify it for federal funds.

University of Chicago

The plan called for the clearing of a strip of land one block deep and one mile in length along the southern boundry of the campus extending from Cottage Grove to Stony Island. The university's plan was to clear the area and extend its campus.

Part of the devastating effect this announcement had on the people of Woodlawn was in the realization that the university had fully developed its urban renewal plan and had already announced it through the news media. With all the university's political and economic power, early approval of the plan from the city government was almost a sure thing.

After the announcement appeared in the paper the feeling throughout the community and especially among the homeowners was, "We are doomed. The university is going to take over all of Woodlawn." There was absolutely no thought in the mind of most of the people of Woodlawn that anything could be done to change the anticipated efforts of the university, because they knew how the university had controlled the Hyde Park-Kenwood urban renewal program. This was typical of the fear and powerlessness that pervades the black communities throughout the nation. Historically, their fears are well grounded. Black people do not have a history of winning victories against the power structure.

Further, the university was no small college. It was a veritable giant. It had over a thousand faculty members, most of whom held Ph.D. degrees or equivalent professional degrees. It held a worldwide reputation as the place where man's first controlled self-sustaining nuclear chain reaction was achieved. It operated such famous institutions as Argonne Laboratories, Argonne Cancer Research Hospital, Albert Merit Billings Hospital, Bobs Roberts Memorial Hospital, Chicago Lying-In Hospital, the Nathan Goldblatt Memorial Hospital, and many clinics. The University of Chicago had a staff of more than 15,000 person and ranked among the ten largest employers in metropolitan Chicago.

The residents of Woodlawn, however, had no reason to love the university. Prior to the middle sixties the university had projects of research and development in such far-off places as Pakistan, yet it spent nothing to relieve poverty in Woodlawn. Typical of so many large universities, it simply ignored the poor in its own back yard. It went further; it even built a barbed-wire barrier against the Woodlawn residents along part of the south side of its campus. Little wonder citizens of the black community grow cynical about America's self-righteous criticism of such affronts to freedom as the Berlin Wall, when they see walls erected everywhere against them by the white Establishment. The university was the ever present, glaring example to Woodlawn residents.

The period immediately following the announcement of the university's urban renewal plan became the most critical period in the early history of TWO. How could despair be transformed into courage? How could apathy be converted into action? There was no time for careful consideration or orderly planning. Leaders of TWO, along with the staff and all available volunteers, moved throughout the community, informing the people of what was happening, focusing and defining the issues and fanning the smoldering fires of anger into a blue flame of action. In a dramatic meeting TWO voted to oppose the University of Chicago's expansion plan. The secretary wrote to Washington stating that because the community had not participated in planning the urban renewal, TWO opposed the plan and demanded it be stopped immediately. This initiated a bitter conflict that lasted from 1961 through 1963. Without The Woodlawn Organization the community would have been powerless to protect itself against the bulldozing power of the giant university.

The Woodlawn Organization never opposed the plan for the expansion of the south campus, per se. TWO did oppose the piecemeal planning for the Woodlawn community that served the interests of outside power structures without benefiting the people of Woodlawn. TWO also opposed the plan because the people of Woodlawn had not been involved in the planning process. The university was expanding into Woodlawn by using the vehicle of urban renewal. Fortunately for Woodlawn, the urban renewal law stated very clearly that there must be citizen participation in plans for urban renewal.

The south campus plan, as it was proposed, benefited the University of Chicago only. It was clear that the cost would be prohibitive if the university were forced to purchase the land privately. Private acquisition would mean that the university would have to run down the titles to all of the buildings in the proposed expansion area that it did not already own and negotiate on an individual basis with individual owners for all properties. After purchasing all of the buildings, the university would have to hire demolition contractors to clear all the land and make it available for the erecting of new buildings. It was far less expensive from the university's point of view to have the area declared slum and blighted and made an urban renewal area. The city could use tax money to purchase the property at condemnation prices, clear the land, and then sell the raw land back to the university for less than a dollar per square foot.

TWO asked to meet with the South East Chicago Commission, a powerful local organization comprised of private individuals with Julian Levi of the University of Chicago as executive director. This commission was the spokesman for the University of Chicago in all matters pertaining to urban renewal. Repeated requests for a meeting with the SECC to negotiate a settlement were refused. To meet with TWO alone would have been tantamount to recognizing TWO as the community organization and spokesman for Woodlawn, which was precisely TWO's claim.

The South East Chicago Commission responded by demanding to meet with all the local groups of Woodlawn. TWO represented over a hundred groups in Woodlawn, and would not go into a meeting with four or five other groups representing practically no one but themselves and in such a meeting be outvoted five to one. At no point, however, would the South East Chicago Commission sit down with TWO alone, and so the battle with the University become a stalemate.

City of Chicago Planning

TWO then turned to city officials and insisted that nothing be done in the south campus area until an over-all renewal plan for Woodlawn could be drawn up with the people of Woodlawn participating on a meaningful level.

In a stormy meeting in the chambers of City Council TWO demanded that the city undertake a survey of the community to ascertain how the entire Woodlawn area could benefit from the university's proposed urban renewal program. The city agreed to do this, and several months later city planners came up with a proposal labeled "For Discussion Purposes Only."

The package was drawn up in typical city fashion, with absolutely no citizen participation. For months TWO had tried to find out what the City Planning Department was doing, but to no avail. Their position seemed to be that the local residents may have an opportunity to express their ideas only after all the plans have been drawn up. This means that the people have only two choices—to oppose the plan or to accept the plan. TWO's philosophy is that the people themselves must be a part of the *entire planning process* from beginning to end. The Woodlawn Organization took a bold step at this point and engaged a group of private city planners to do a critique of the city of Chicago's proposal and to propose alternatives to it.

This tactic put the city of Chicago in the middle of the conflict. The city had run out of funds for urban renewal programs and wanted the $14 million from Section 112 of the Housing Act of 1959.[1] For the city to receive this money the University of Chicago had to sign certification papers. The university would not sign those papers until the city produced some kind of urban renewal program that would guarantee the university the land needed for the south campus. This the city could not do, because the people of the community were not in favor of the university's plan as it then existed and had vetoed it.

At this point TWO felt that powerful segments of the white society were closing in on it. The *Christian Century,* a well-known religious periodical, joined forces with the University of Chicago and bitterly attacked The Woodlawn Organization, the Industrial Areas Foundation, and the Roman Catholic Church in an editorial dated May 10, 1961. The editorial quoted largely

[1]The University of Chicago, working in consort with 20 universities in 1959, was able to persuade Congress to enact Section 112 of the Housing Act of 1959, which provided in effect that when a university had spent its own funds in acquisition of properties for campus expansion in accordance with an approved grant, those expenditures upon certification by the university would be recognized as local non-cash-grants-in-aide for the benefit of the municipality. Hence, a city assisting a university in the expansion of its campus could secure matching federal funds without cost to the city.

from an article by Ruth Moore in the *Chicago Sun Times* interpreting the conflict in terms of open or closed cities. Miss Moore and *The Christian Century* accused TWO of a program that "in its own words is to rub raw the sores of discontent and to rouse dormant hostilities," of a "passion for keeping masses of people from being 'redeveloped out' of their slums," and of being used by the Roman Catholic Church to delay integration of nearby white Catholic areas. Miss Moore pictured the University of Chicago as working for open cities and humane progress along with most of the Protestant churches in the area. The *Christian Century* charged that the church was identifying with the demagogic methods of the IAF, and that the Protestant ministers and leaders were not being true to their Christian commitment in that they were forsaking "the promotion of voluntary cooperation and the concept of the open city, both of which are implicit in the Christian gospel, advocating instead salvation through compulsion practiced through predatory power structures dominating closed cities. . . ."

TWO reacted to this as an irresponsible and misleading piece of journalism. It was filled with innuendo, half-truths, and misleading statements. The spokesman for TWO categorically denied the editorial's charges against the organization. He also questioned the statement about the university's working for an open society on the basis of the Hyde Park-Kenwood urban renewal project, and suggested that the cause of justice would have been better served had these remarks about closed cities been directed at the Chicago Real Estate Board.

The Public Relations Office of the University of Chicago tried to persuade several daily newspapers in Chicago to make something of the fact that the Catholic Church supported Saul Alinsky and the work of the IAF in Woodlawn. The newspapers refused to be a part of the matter, so the material was published in the Chicago *Maroon,* the student weekly paper. Dr. Joseph Sitler, a member of the faculty of the University of Chicago's Divinity School, called the article an irresponsible piece of journalism and formally protested its publication.

Charles Silberman in his book *Crisis in Black and White* supported Dr. Sitler's position and went on to say:

> University officials apparently have regarded the Church as an enemy ever since 1958, when Monsignor John Egan, Executive

> Director of the Cardinal's Committee on Community Organization and Urban Renewal, criticized the then-pending Hyde Park-Kenwood urban renewal program. Monsignor Egan saw the program, quite rightly, as a venture in Negro removal; he pointed out that plans called for demolition of a great deal of adequate housing occupied largely by Negroes, and that few of these residents would be able to afford the new apartments and houses that were to be erected. . . .
>
> In any event, the Woodlawn Organization certainly was not the product of any Papist conspiracy. On the contrary, the organization represents one of the most meaningful examples of Protestant-Catholic co-operation to be found anywhere in the United States. . . . The result has been the collaboration of the Archdiocese, the Chicago Presbytery, and the Church Federation of Chicago. The involvement of church leaders of all denominations in social action to improve the Negro's lot is TWO's most enduring contribution.[5]

TWO did not take a purely negative stance toward the University of Chicago's problem, but made positive recommendations. One of these, which was finally accepted, was that a portion of the $14 million in federal credits should be used to benefit the people of Woodlawn. TWO further proposed that three blocks of deteriorated commercial structures, from 60th to 63rd streets on Cottage Grove Avenue, be demolished and that new low-cost, low-rise housing be erected in their place. There would be very little relocation of families because the area was basically composed of dilapidated and deteriorated communal structures. It was because of the minimum need for relocation that TWO recommended the site.

TWO recommended 221 (D) 3 housing because at that time (1961-1963) it was thought throughout the country to be the kind of housing poor people could afford. (It has since been discovered that 221 (D) 3 is not the panacea everyone thought it was at that time.)

Mayor Daley broke the stalemate in 1963. He called a meeting of TWO representatives and representatives from the University of Chicago. This meeting and another subsequent one firmly estab-

---

[5]Charles Silberman, *Crisis in Black and White* (New York: Random House, 1964), pp. 340 ff.

lished the right of the people to participate in the planning of their community.

The mayor agreed to several points:

> (1) A citizen's committee would be appointed by the mayor to deal with urban renewal in Woodlawn.
>
> (2) TWO would have a majority of members on the committee.
>
> (3) The deteriorated commercial structures on Cottage Grove between 60th and 63rd streets would be demolished and low-cost, low-rise (but not public) housing would be erected by a non-profit corporation.
>
> (4) No buildings on south campus would be demolished until the land on Cottage Grove was cleared and new construction begun.
>
> (5) The person appointed as administrator for urban renewal would have to be acceptable to TWO.

After the struggle over south campus was won in principle, slow, faltering improvements took place in relations between the university and TWO. Reconciliation was slow to come. The struggle had been long and bitter. Mistrust on both sides left deep scars, which to this day have not completely disappeared. Reconciliation is occurring, however, and it is most evident in the mutual support and working relationships that have been built during the development of TWO's model cities plan.

Some residual effects of the earlier struggle still remain. Many Woodlawn people are still convinced that the university is not truly concerned with the welfare of Woodlawn residents. Many believe that the university has hidden plans to take over the entire community via the bulldozer, with no concern for the human problem that would be left in its wake. This nagging suspicion is a hindrance to full cooperation, and everything possible must be done by the university to demonstrate that it is not biding its time before turning Woodlawn into the southern part of its physical plant.

The Woodlawn Organization decided that not only should it be in on the planning of this first urban renewal battle but the community ought to help plan the development of new housing as well. Since the 221 (D) 3 housing could be built with federal financing, TWO felt that with the proper assistance it could develop the Cottage Grove land.

TWO sent a proposal for rehabilitation to Victor De Grazia, Executive Vice President of the Kate Maremont Foundation. This foundation was active in rehabilitation work in the ghettos of Chicago. TWO needed seed money for engaging architects to draw plans for the development of the site and to process the proposal to its completion. Since this could be federally financed, all seed money spent by the foundation would be returned to the foundation. The foundation was interested in this proposal and agreed to make the seed money available.

A separate corporation, The Woodlawn Organization–Kate Maremont Development Association, resulted. To insure community control of the project TWO would always have the chairmanship of the board of directors as well as the majority of the board members. When the Cottage Grove land was put up for bid the new development association's bid was accepted. At this writing the corporation is beginning to build 502 housing units on the site.

Chapter Six

Urban Education Developmental Project

There is a great deal of evidence to show that inner-city schools of the kind found in the Woodlawn area are not educating many of the children whom they serve. Teachers and administrators may try, but they do not get through to ghetto children. Proof of this lies in the low levels of achievement of the children and in the large number of dropouts. Children who grow up in communities such as Woodlawn are unprepared to learn what school has to offer. They see little relationship between what happens inside the school and outside the school. As long as ghetto schools operate as if they served only the white middle-class society they will fail to reach ghetto children.

This chapter is the story of the collaboration between The Woodlawn Organization, the Chicago Public Schools, and the University of Chicago. What makes it so remarkable is that only a few short years before the beginning of this school project TWO and the University of Chicago were locked in combat over the problem of urban renewal. The new relationship between TWO and the university illustrates in a dramatic way that conflict and confrontation can be resolved creatively and can lead to reconciliation and collaboration.

The University of Chicago began to take seriously its responsibility to the Woodlawn neighborhood lying just south of the campus. Previously the university had been active in research and development in projects scattered far and wide over the earth but had ignored the massive problems at its doorstep. In his commencement address in the winter quarter of 1965, however, Edward Levi, the university provost, made a statement that represented a major commitment to improving ghetto schools:

> We must rethink the university's participation in the training of scholars for public service, not losing the inhibitions which guided us, but recognizing this as one of the missions of scholars, and that in some areas, of which the education of the underprivileged is one, and, in a quite different way, international studies program is another, greater involvement is required both for training and research.

Urban Research and Development Center

The university developed a proposal for a research and development center in urban education. Through this center the university planned to study and work with the public schools, and with the neighborhoods that contained such schools, particularly the Woodlawn neighborhood. Once again, however, the proposal lacked the basic ingredient of collaboration with the Woodlawn community and the public schools. It was essentially a unilateral development on the part of the university.

On May 4, 1966, the Office of Education conducted a site visit, relative to the research and development center.

After the visit, TWO asked to review a copy of the proposal and responded with the following statement:

> The Woodlawn Organization proposes that collaboration on a proposed program be on the basis of respect for the self-determination of the greater Woodlawn community. TWO's feeling in this regard is based on its history, with which the University is in a large part familiar, and on our conviction that research without the willing, close participation of the indigenous community will be ineffective and false research.

This letter stimulated the University of Chicago to view its conflict of interests with TWO as an opportunity for dialogue and potential collaboration. Shortly the university received the report of the site visit of the Office of Education indicating that three changes had to be made in the proposal before it would be approved. From TWO's perspective the most important one was that the "cooperation and participation" of local community groups would have to be secured, and the university would have to work closely with community organizations and with the existing elementary and secondary schools in District 14 of the Chicago public school system. TWO was interested in working with the university when meaningful citizen participation and involvement could occur at every level of the program.

Representatives of the three institutions worked out specific mechanisms for cooperative effort. The three groups appointed a joint council of twenty-one members, the Woodlawn Community Board, which consisted of seven representatives each from the Woodlawn neighborhood, the Chicago Public Schools, and the University of Chicago. TWO insisted on appointing the seven representatives from Woodlawn since TWO was the only umbrella organization in Woodlawn. TWO also insisted that the community would have a veto on any given issue. The university and the Chicago Public Schools agreed as long as they too could veto. It was further agreed that any one of the three groups would be permitted to caucus before the vote was taken.

The Woodlawn Community Board was successfully forged, but not without the heat of conflict. Hardly had the board begun to enjoy the experience of being successfully welded together when another problem developed—whether or not the entire District 14 should be included in the experimental district. District 14 includes not only East Woodlawn, but also the Hyde Park-Kenwood community immediately to the north of the university campus. Hyde Park-Kenwood also has a community conference. TWO was opposed from the very beginning to working with representatives of Hyde Park-Kenwood, because the Board of Education had decided to build a separate new high school in Hyde Park-Kenwood rather than to reconstruct the high school located in Woodlawn, which had served all of District 14.

Dean Campbell of the School of Education of the University of Chicago indicated that he did not favor changing the structure of the Woodlawn Community Board in any way. He agreed that if the university wished to work with Hyde Park-Kenwood it would need another and separate structure, perhaps similar to the Woodlawn Community Board. Although Curtis Melnick, superintendent of District 14, at first desired to have the whole of District 14 as an experimental district, TWO insisted that Hyde Park-Kenwood should not be involved in planning for Woodlawn nor should Woodlawn have a voice in the Hyde Park-Kenwood planning. Further, many children eligible to participate in Title I poverty programs are found in Woodlawn, but few are found in Hyde Park-Kenwood. Levi, Melnick, and TWO finally agreed to include only the Woodlawn area.

A project that started out to be an urban research and development center located on the campus of the university made a dramatic shift toward working with the schools with the complete cooperation of the community in which the schools were found. This decentralization vividly portrayed the growing commitment of the university to work on the problems of ghetto education.

Four months passed during which time the staff of the Woodlawn Community Board prepared a revised proposal for a developmental project, which was submitted to the Office of Education on September 13. Late in November a letter was received from the Office of Education indicating that its Bureau of Research would not fund the proposal. The rejection was a severe blow to the young community board. At the meeting in which this rejection was received the TWO spokesman made the following statement: "I see this as a rejection and I am not happy about it. This decision hurts the children in Woodlawn and in urban areas beyond. This is the time to fight this decision or to redraft the proposal to cause Washington to have a different point of view." Julian Levi suggested that the discussions on the proposal be reopened with the government at the highest level. This suggestion eventually was unanimously recommended by the Woodlawn Community Board.

These two critical decisions—the one to work independently of the Hyde Park-Kenwood Community Council, and the second to press for funding of a project for the Woodlawn Community Board—did much to establish the board as a cohesive unit. It is curious that the Office of Education stimulated the creative conflict from which collaboration emerged.

Approval of Woodlawn Community Board Project

It was fascinating and even awesome to watch the System swing into action to achieve results desired by men in power. Within two months after having its proposed developmental project rejected, the university received a letter from the Office of Education indicating governmental approval of the developmental project at a support level of approximately $70,000. This reversal was brought about by the university's Dean of the Graduate School of Education, Roald Campbell, who directed letters to John Gardner, Secretary of Health, Education and Welfare, and to Commissioner of Education Harold Howe, asking for a review of the decision by the Office of Education. The appeal was granted and the project was funded. Without doubt the System works well for men who wield power.

The community board appointed a project staff: Willard Congreve of the university, project director; Anthony C. Gibbs of TWO and Lorraine M. Lavigne of the Chicago Public Schools, associate directors; and staff assistants from all three organizations. The project staff was given major responsibility for creating and developing ideas for the planning project that had just been funded.

The staff drew up a tentative draft of a general statement of purpose and procedures and submitted it to the Woodlawn Community Board. The first draft included this statement:

> The Woodlawn Organization is primarily interested in building leadership for the redevelopment of the community and in changing basic educational program so that it will be geared to the special needs of the youth of the community.

Since TWO was really interested in a basic change in the educational system and not just in the special needs of youth that might be met with superficial or compensatory educational programs, TWO insisted that the staff change the statement to read:

> The Woodlawn Organization is primarily interested in building leadership for the redevelopment of the community and in changing the basic educational program and the allocation of resources so that the educational system will be geared to the needs of the youth and the community.

This new statement allows the development of programs that give the black person a better understanding of himself and his contribution to the growth of the American society. Many blacks labor under a burden of self-hatred. Few materials used in schools do justice to the contribution the black man has made to his country. Further, the Negroes pictured and discussed in textbooks are those who are acceptable to whites. This entire concept must change. The board understood this and approved the new statement.

The Assessment of Problems

The next major task of the project staff was to provide an assessment of problems, including the perceptions and opinions of persons in school, in the neighborhood, and on the university campus. This assessment program was one of the most severe tests of the collaborative efforts of the Woodlawn Community Board. It required that the public school system look at itself and open itself to public scrutiny by representatives of TWO and the university. This put a serious responsibility on both the university and on TWO to act with the utmost integrity, in view of the implicit threat to the schools posed by the assessment program.

The assessment was designed with as much scientific rigor as possible. The project staff designed a structured interview schedule designed to elicit opinions about what problems existed in the schools as well as suggestions to solve these problems. Randomly selected children, parents, teachers, and school staff members, in addition to principals of three elementary schools, one upper-grade center, and one high school, were the respondents in the study. An open-ended interview, with questions designed to release a free flow of thoughts from the respondents, proved valuable. The responses were categorized systematically, and the findings put into a written report.

The project staff did uncover many promising programs in the schools. The problems, however, were overwhelming, and the means for dealing with them cruelly insufficient. In the administrative domain there were frequently sighted deficiencies in floor space, furniture, and instructional materials. Libraries were either undersized or nonexistent. Recreation and relaxation areas for both student and staff were sighted as being woefully inadequate.

The report indicated that the role of the teacher had changed so much and there were so many nonteaching tasks that it was hard for a teacher to recognize herself as a teacher. There was great need for more qualified adults to work with the children. The teachers needed more help in the classroom from specialists than they were getting. Administrative decisions were often made without consulting the people in the schools whom the decisions affected.

Findings with respect to teaching and learning indicated that conditions in the home and community were detrimental to school learning. The presence of gangs in the community was cited as a major deterrent to learning. Some parents were apathetic and hostile toward school. Their value orientation was different from that of the teachers. Other parents criticized principals and teachers for lack of interest in the ghetto child and parent.

Criticisms were advanced about the lack of program versatility, and the lack of attention to aspects of life that are particularly important to the black person; and programs were seen as being too oriented toward college.

Teachers came under criticism because of poor discipline in their classroom, for sometimes punishing the underachiever and the slow learner just as if these children were behavior problems, for lacking effective techniques for motivating students.

Teachers reported that children came to them inadequately prepared for reading, speaking, and listening, making it impossible for them to perform at a certain grade level.

Although reporting the assessment findings to the Woodlawn Community Board was a difficult public experience for the Chicago Public Schools, the men from the schools demonstrated at the reporting meeting, perhaps more then at any time previously, their desire to collaborate on school improvement. They listened to the problems presented, and accepted in large measure the pressures that had been generated from the critique. At the conclusion of the report one of the principals replied, "I can't quarrel with the data or the categories. We principals are sensitive because we are in the field, but the school has to be changed somehow."

Collaboration for the Improvement of Schools

To indicate that the Woodlawn Community Board was not just another board, and that the study it had conducted was not "just another study," the project staff helped teachers reassess the afterschool reading program. They decided to continue to support it as it stood rather than reallocating funds from it to a new program. Second, the project staff helped alleviate a dire shortage of substitute teachers in Woodlawn schools by developing an experimental substitute teacher program. A third short-range project was a film-making project designed to reveal the nature of existing relationships among home, school, and community through the lives of individual children.

With the short-range program moving ahead, the staff began to look toward some long-range programs. The project staff became increasingly aware of the need for a major overhaul of the structure of the schools if eventual success were to be realized. The staff soon found themselves wrestling with the need to develop and appropriate an administrative plan that would permit such change. Several attempts were made to design either a program or a structure into which the program could be fitted.

The staff produced a major document containing five sections: a review of the assessment findings, a summary of the philosophical and psychological basis for overhauling the social system of the school, a suggested strategy for bringing about the change that was needed, a description of the focus for the experiment encapsulated in the phrase "people helping people," and a discussion of alternative administrative designs for collaborative action.

For the first time in its history at one of the meetings of the Woodlawn Community Board a caucus was called for. The board faced the major issue of whether to include all the schools in East Woodlawn or only one stream of schools from K through 12. If the experimental project would focus on a stream of schools the experiment would be large enough to have validity and small enough to be controllable. Some schools, however, might feel left out, with a resulting decline in morale. Over this question the representatives of the Chicago Public Schools needed an opportunity to convene privately.

At the conclusion of the caucus the Chicago Public School people said they could accept an experimental stream of schools, but in addition they would like to see a reading readiness program at the preschool or kindergarten level for *all* the elementary schools in East Woodlawn. The school people insisted that all the schools in the district needed something to keep up their morale. Consensus was reached on a motion to establish a stream of experimental schools, and also to allocate money to the rest of the schools in the East Woodlawn neighborhood with the individual school staff determining how to spend these funds.

The board concurred in the recommendation of the project staff to retain the tripartite collaborative administrative structure established through the Woodlawn Community Board, and the staff was now free to work out a detailed proposal for the program in the experimental schools.

The legal question of the public schools' delegating their responsibility to other groups had next to be solved. By statutory law this was impossible. A solution was found in an agreement whereby an experimental program designed for the schools in Woodlawn would be shunted through the Woodlawn Community Board for approval before going to the General Superintendent for his approval.

The Woodlawn Community Board created an experimental school district that met the legal specifications and statutory responsibilities of the School District of Chicago. The Chicago School Board and the Woodlawn Community Board hammered out a memorandum of agreement in two weeks of intensified work to meet the deadline for submitting a proposal for the experimental school district of Woodlawn for Title III funding.

Chapter Seven

TWO and Woodlawn Youth

The Woodlawn Organization attempted to come to grips with the most significant problem in the ghettos across the nation—alienated youth. White America has no answer to this problem other than a reflex demand for the use of force. The Woodlawn Organization sponsored a program that would begin to deal with the problem. The program was designed by Jerome Bernstein who was at this time Deputy Director, Manpower Division, Citizen Action Programs, Office of Economic Opportunity, Washington. The program had several unorthodox features in it, however, that made it unacceptable to the white power structure. The project was controversial; but when judged by criteria established in the initial proposal, it was successful. TWO's efforts were thwarted, however; the project was eventually killed by the white political structure, all the way from city hall to a U.S. senatorial committee.

The fundamental philosophy of TWO is that the only long-range solution to problems in ghetto communities in this country is for the people in these communities to solve the problems themselves by exercising their own self-determination. Engagement in real issues restores human dignity. That same philosophy, it was felt, would succeed with youth, because young people demand not just freedom from imposed authority, but a structure within which they can change their own destiny and at the same time know that the adults in the community support them.

One of the principal reasons why young people organize into groups called "gangs" outside the ghetto is to deal with the chaotic conditions with which they are confronted in the ghetto. The group is the only vehicle they have for gaining real power, security, and socioeconomic status. The gang is a marginal social structure created to attain legitimate goals by whatever means possible. The Woodlawn Organization felt that it was quite possible to help the youth groups in Woodlawn redirect their energies into positive, constructive programs to attain their goals, and that such programs would be of direct and immediate benefit not only to them, but to the entire community as well.

Programs designed to meet the problems of youth in the urban ghetto, besides being miserably few in number, also typically operate on a narrow recreational base. They are usually carried out through established youth-service agencies. It is precisely because these agencies are bound by traditional rules and regulations designed for a different clientele that they do not adequately meet the needs of a new population. Most ghetto youth view such agency programs as irrelevant and paternalistic. The result is that those most in need of the service are screened out or screen themselves out and remain both physically and psychologically alienated from the agency.

TWO has an established history of close contact with the poor, with unemployed and alienated members of the community, as well as a history of creating and operating successful programs. TWO had both the closeness to the street and the administrative background necessary to carry out this new program for urban-ghetto youth. The target population of the youth program was comprised of eight hundred out-of-school, unemployed youth in the Woodlawn area. The program endeavored to recruit youth who were not members of any youth organization, as well as those who were members of youth organizations. The age of program participants ranged from sixteen to twenty-five.

Youth Organizations—The Gangs

It is important to note that the youth groups do not refer to themselves as gangs, but call themselves youth organizations. They see a gang as a large disorganized mass or mob, and they feel that they are highly organized groups. When the writer refers to these organizations as gangs, he does so only because of the reader's own orientation.

Many of Woodlawn's youth belong to one of two basic organizations, the Blackstone Rangers or the Eastside Disciples. The estimated membership of the Blackstone Rangers is approximately three thousand youth ranging from ages thirteen through twenty-five; the membership of the Disciples is approximately one thousand. Woodlawn Avenue is the basic dividing line between the two "turfs."

The Eastside Disciples is an affiliate of a larger youth organization located principally in the Englewood community. There is a formal structural line between the two groups, but the chain of command is not rigidly formal. It is normally rather loose, except in the event of a total gang crisis.

The Eastside Disciples were first seen in the community of Woodlawn after a parade on "Bud Billikin's Day." On this occasion there was a major confrontation between the Disciples and the Blackstone Rangers. During 1965 there were only verbal scrimmages between the two rival groups, yet this was enough to crystallize "turf" boundaries and leadership identification.

The Eastside Disciples generally consider their turf boundaries to run from 60th to 67th Street and from Cottage Grove to Woodlawn Avenue. The members range in age from twelve to twenty years. There are approximately 150 key members, but the larger Disciples body numbers approximately a thousand youth. A very few are married and have families. They are all male, with no apparent female auxiliary group. The governing body is composed of ten council members. It is their responsibility to advise, but in most instances they carry out the functions of the leader. The Eastside Disciples are a smaller, less organizationally sophisticated group of youth than are the Blackstone Rangers.

The Blackstone Rangers were identified as a "gang" in Woodlawn around 1964. They are a powerful group, effectively organized. They interact with the rest of Woodlawn, as well as with the numerous organizations and agencies within the city that touch the members' lives. The successes of the organization have resulted in providing both the membership and the nonmember related groups with protection, prestige, and hope—things that no agency, the community, family, or program has been able to do.

The Rangers steadily increased in numbers and developed their organizational style, until by 1966 they numbered approximately one thousand members. The members range in age from twelve to twenty-three. The older members may be married or unmarried. The Rangers organization functions with rules and regulations and norms of expected behavior. A small group of members called the "heavies" or "chiefs," a group numbering twenty-one youths who are referred to collectively as the Main Twenty-one, are between eighteen and twenty-three years of age.

Females are involved in a related group called the Rangerettes. Another group of youth under twelve years of age are called the Peewees. They are not members, but the Rangers plan and carry out various activities for them. These youngsters live in the same violent community as do the Rangers.

Great animosity existed between the Rangers and the Disciples. Members of each gang were restricted to their own turf by the other gang. This put certain schools, viaducts, railroad crossings, and recreational facilities off-limits. Prior to the start of the youth program, this animosity was so severe that murders, shootings, knifings, and beatings resulted.

Here is a sample of incidents of violence during the month of April, 1966: On the night of April 10 a youth was shot on the street. On the same night another youth was shot at another location. On the morning of April 14 a youth was shot in front of the school store at 62nd Street and Stoney Island Avenue. On April 14, in the evening, another youth was assaulted by eight youths whose ages were between 15 and 17. On the evening of the next day a youth was shot at the Woodlawn Boy's Club by an unidentified assailant. On April 18, a youth was shot at 62nd and Woodlawn by an unnamed assailant. On April 22, in the afternoon, there was a gang fight at 60th Street and University Avenue. Thirteen youths were arrested and police confiscated two knives, one homemade gun, one whip, one blackjack, and several ropes.

While no one would say that every incident of violence enumerated was perpetrated by the Blackstone Rangers or the Eastside Disciples, violence between the two youth groups was so frequent that the entire Woodlawn community was alarmed.

Chicago newspapers carried stories headlined in the following way: POLICE WORRIED BY BUILD-UP OF GANGS—

MORE TEEN VIOLENCE HITS HYDE PARK HIGH—3,000 TEENS WILL CLOSE CHICAGO—YOUTH STRIVE TO CURB TEEN VIOLENCE—SCHOOLS CLOSE AMIDST THREAT OF SUMMER TEEN VIOLENCE—SIX MORE TEEN GANGSTERS WOUND HALF DOZEN RIVALS—WEEK'S SCORE: 33 HURT, 2 DEAD.

In the afternoon of July 21, 1966, the Blackstone Rangers and the Eastside Disciples had a peace conference with Police Superintendent O. W. Wilson, and Commander William Griffin of the 3rd Police District, which includes the Woodlawn area. It was announced in the newspapers and on television that a truce between the two youth organizations had been effected. On the same evening at 8:40 p.m. the truce broke down and six youths were shot.

Throughout this entire early period of 1966, there was not active in Woodlawn one preventive program aimed at alienated youth. Later neighborhood agencies and churches in the community attempted to resolve the problems of the gangs, and several programs were instituted to discourage the growth of gangs and the disruptive activities of these youth. Over and over again, however, these programs failed to attack the roots of the problem, namely the alienation, the economic insecurity of the youth, and the suffocation of ghetto life.

The gang members looked upon the representatives of the institutions of the community as being insincere and full of social-work clichés. To these youth, police and school personnel represent hostile authority figures; and gang members act out their feelings toward such authority in hostile ways. They view the community of Woodlawn as their "hood," and the boundaries of their "turf" become the walls of their prison and of their sanctuary.

The present scientific literature on youth subculture and delinquency is inadequate to describe the nature of a group like the Rangers. Rather than being a small gang, serving primarily as a replacement for a family, the Rangers are more truly urban in character. That is, while the group operates with both formal and informal structures, it is not a primary group. Relationships within the organization are necessarily secondary and the organization functions more like a huge bureaucratic organization, since more than a thousand members are involved.

The organizational style of the Rangers represents an emerging type among informal, social organizations in urban areas. The methods of dealing with crisis, the reaching of decisions, the unique combination of personal and bureaucratic forms of operation indicate the nature of the organization and the necessity of its members to rely on a framework not usually associated with informal social groups. For example, rather than a single leader, the leadership of the organization rests with twenty-one persons. The leadership unit operates a good deal like a board of control. Individual members of the organizations do not know every other member by first name, although they know some members on this basis. Members generally know one another only as a Ranger. Unilateral action taken by a member or a particular subgroup is not condoned by the organization. Although leaders do make on-the-spot decisions when necessary, the organization, through its board of control, acts formally at predetermined meetings with something like an agenda, to decide what action is appropriate. It is the organization that commits the act, not the individual. Organizational norms indicate the degree to which a member's behavior is prescribed, prohibited, recommended, or permitted.

The development of this type of organization illustrates the point that while Blackstone Rangers are not formally educated, the leadership and many of its members are sophisticated in the sense of building a workable, meaningful organization in a ghetto in the city. When a member has been affiliated with the Rangers for some time, his loyalties lie with the organization rather than with the home or with any other type of agency or organization.

Pressures to destroy the organization have been frequent but unsuccessful. The normal attrition that characterizes many kinds of informal gangs does not apply to the Rangers. The youth's identity in the ghetto and outside of it is intimately tied to his membership in his organization, and even when he assumes family responsibilities he maintains his membership.

The identity of the youth in Woodlawn with the organization becomes critical with respect to the various city and federal programs that are designed to assist the youth in the ghetto. There are several reasons why the programs failed to have an impact on the Rangers. First, most programs, either by accident or by design, require that a member make a choice between his group or the program. When confronted with that choice, the youth opts for his group. Membership in the group represents one of the few successful experiences he has had during his life in the ghetto. The youth organization does not permit participation in traditional social service programs, primarily because the proposed program offers no real solution to the difficulties confronting the membership.

A second reason for the failure of traditional programs is that they often appear to be unrelated to the youth organization's major concerns. When an agency offers some sort of training program, the individual may not be interested in it if he sees that it is unlikely to accomplish his stated objectives, or if he perceives that when he completes the program he has no guarantee of employment.

Third, the program is always "offered" to the youths by an agency. The youth organization plays no part in the design of the program and individuals must participate in the proposed program on the terms as set forth by the agency offering it. The program is never designed to take into account the existing relationships within the youth organizations, nor does the agency seek the organization's approval. Since the youth's organization is not considered important enough to include in the program design, the individual members are likely to be unsympathetic to the program and to its objectives. Moreover, what some adults think are appropriate programs for ghetto youth are rarely what the group perceives as its needs. Most programs are relatively limited in scope and duration, and involve only a small number of the group's members. Since these groups have by contrast developed a highly sophisticated organizational structure, the programs appropriate to them will require new approaches and creative components.

Fourth, the various programs fail to capitalize upon the nature of the youth organizations and to take into account the functions it performs for its members. Because ghetto youth organizations are generally perceived as antisocial gangs and detrimental to the welfare of the community, there is little empathy with the larger objectives of the organization.

Much has been said and written about the difficulty of identifying the indigenous leadership in the ghetto areas. In such groups as the Rangers and the Disciples, the leadership role is evident.

The new style of organization represented by the Blackstone Rangers and the Eastside Disciples indicates that youth in the ghetto have been able to build meaningful organizations based primarily upon personal relationships with bureaucratic structures, but still preserving significant interpersonal dimensions.

A rift began to develop within The Woodlawn Organization over the problem of gangs. A few groups felt that the only answer was more police protection. These groups were so overwhelmed by fear that they were ready to condone any method whatever to calm the situation. They were ready to endorse police brutality, indiscriminate jailing of youth, and a general violation of the civil rights of the citizens of the community. Their only concern was "stop the violence." It did not seem to matter to them how it was done.

The vast majority of the members of The Woodlawn Organization rejected that philosophy. They knew that something had to be done, but they were not ready to set aside the Bill of Rights and the Constitution of the United States, let alone break the spirit of hundreds of youth.

TWO understood to some degree the antisocial behavior of the gangs. It is precisely for this reason that TWO could develop a viable alternative to the bleak future of gang members. Many obstacles lay in the path, but TWO felt that these obstacles could be overcome.

The staff of TWO met with representatives of the President's Committee on Juvenile Delinquency, faculty members of the University of Chicago, staff members of the National Institute on Mental Health, Leon Sullivan of the Opportunities Industrialization Center in Philadelphia, and staff members of the Ford Foundation, to study the subject of alienated youth. TWO reached two specific conclusions as a result of these consultations: (1) The greatest need of the youth of Woodlawn was a job training program. (2) No program would likely succeed with these young men unless it involved the gang leadership in the planning, design, and operation of the program. Establishing a means of involving gang leadership was harder.

Relationship with the Rangers was tenuous, to say the least. Relationship with the Disciples was almost nonexistent. TWO had worked with these groups when riots were taking place on the west side. Staff people had encouraged them to work to keep violence out of Woodlawn and to that end had assisted them in whatever way they could. The Woodlawn Organization, however, had no in-depth relationship with either of the youth groups.

TWO decided to attempt the development of a project that would involve the two major youth groups. TWO contacted Rev. John Fry, pastor of the First Presbyterian Church of Chicago. Prior to Rev. Fry's coming to Chicago, First Presbyterian Church had played a dynamic role in community affairs in Woodlawn. Under the co-pastorate of Dr. Ulysses Blakely and Dr. Charles Leber, the First Presbyterian Church had played a key role in the formation of The Woodlawn Organization and had contributed tremendously to TWO's vitality and growth. Both Dr. Blakely and Dr. Leber had moved on to administrative posts in the Presbyterian Church.

Upon assuming the pastorate of First Presbyterian Church in 1965, Rev. Fry plunged into community activity. It was not long before he became interested in one of the youth groups in Woodlawn, the Blackstone Rangers. His interest and concern in them deepened, and it culminated in the Blackstone Rangers making their headquarters in the First Presbyterian Church. A section of the third floor of the church was set aside for them and it was here that they had their meetings. They also enjoyed some recreation in the church gymnasium.

Even though the Blackstone Rangers and the Eastside Disciples continued to clash over the issue of "turf," both youth organizations demonstrated a desire to protect the community from riots. During the rioting on Chicago's west side in 1966, the Chicago *Daily Defender* headlined the following: PEACE FOR WOODLAWN; SOUTHSIDE GANG JOINS COPS TO PREVENT FRESH RIOTING. The accompanying *Defender* article read as follows:

> Woodlawn Gang Leaders and Third District Police Officials have joined forces to prevent Westside rioting from spilling over into the tense Woodlawn area. A policeman said, "No members of either of Woodlawn's two major gangs were found to be on the Westside during the riots."

The *Defender* article went on to quote one of the leaders as saying:

> "We don't want a riot. We are trying to get people not to riot. We know we can't win fighting the police and the National Guard. For the last three days, we have been working with police trying to keep down any incidents that might lead to a riot. . . . People say our gang has been on the Westside in the riot—that is not true. All anyone would have to do is to ask people in the neighborhood, and they would find out that our gang has been on the Southside all the time. If our gang wanted a riot, we could start one right here. We don't have to go over to the Westside. But we don't want a riot and we are trying to get people not to riot."

The youth organizations also exhibited an ability and a willingness to involve themselves as a group in social issues. For example, in July of 1966, the Rangers organized five busloads of their members to go to Soldiers Field to support Dr. Martin Luther King, Jr. at an open-air rally, the purpose of which was to protest segregation in education and in housing. They also participated at various times in block and neighborhood clean-up campaigns. Another example of how an attempt at positive action by the Blackstone Rangers resulted in maintaining the organization is illustrated by the Ranger "Bud Billikin's Day" activities. Bud Billikin's Day, celebrating a mythical Chicago figure, is the traditional day on which all past major conflicts have occurred between the Rangers and the Disciples. To the police, Bud Billikin's Day has more potential for a serious riot than any other day in the summer. Two weeks before Bud Billikin's Day, the leadership of the Rangers decided to hold a picnic on that day. The idea was to hold the picnic out of town, since the leadership was convinced that the organization would not survive a major conflict. A meeting was called with representatives of the Urban Progress Center, the Commission on Youth Welfare, and the Chicago Police Department to discuss the possibility of obtaining a grant for buses and food. All agreed to provide the buses and food. The rangers took eight hundred youth to the picnic at the University of Notre Dame, and the activity was carried out without a single incident. The Rangers had taken some positive action in this situation. The circumstances had been analyzed carefully in order to understand the nature of the crisis and to consider the possible alternatives for action.

In addition to facing the riot crisis, the leaders of these youth groups needed time to plan programs for their organization's membership. Although the leadership knew that the members needed some type of basic education program, as well as a vocational-technical program, they lacked the resources and the knowledge about the possibilities of such programs. The leadership also desired to have some voice in determining how the program was to be operated. The leaders were aware that they needed professionals with substantive knowledge and skills, but they wanted to participate in a selection of the professionals who would interact with the members. They felt it was important to know how a professional person in the program would feel about black people in general and the Blackstone Rangers and the Eastside Disciples in particular. They wanted to ensure that the professionals participating in the program would be empathetic with the organization and could accept the culture it represented within the community.

Both the Rangers and the Disciples had to know more about the community if they were to continue to interact positively within it. To understand the organizations and agencies that affect the lives of ghetto people and to recognize the services that they provide were of prime importance.

At that time, Rev. Fry was the one person in Woodlawn who knew the Blackstone Rangers best. TWO asked him to arrange a meeting of TWO and the Ranger leadership to discuss with them the possibility of their participating in a project drawn up by The Woodlawn Organization. TWO also wanted to assure them that their suggestions and their ideas would have a meaningful part in the planning of the project. It was to be their program as well as TWO's program.

While in the process of drawing up the program TWO contacted several institutions and foundations in an effort to interest them. Jerome Bernstein, who was deputy director of the manpower division of the Office of Economic Opportunity, Community Action Programs section, received an abstract of this proposal. He sent word that he was coming to Chicago to look over the situation and to ascertain for himself whether TWO's contact with the youth groups in Woodlawn was of such a nature as to make the kind of proposed program possible.

While this was going on, TWO was trying to make contact with the Eastside Disciples. The Disciples did not have a church or a permanent minister working with them as did the Blackstone Rangers, so making contact with them was a little more difficult. The TWO Staff Director, Leon Finney, received information that a Mr. Cox worked with the Disciple leadership and would arrange to set up a meeting. TWO contacted Cox, explained to him what it was planning, and asked him if he would arrange a meeting with TWO and the Disciple leadership.

Several days later, TWO met with the leaders of the Disciples and explained to them the desire to involve the Disciples and the Rangers in an experimental program. We wanted them to participate in the development of the program. We wanted their ideas and their views. We also wanted an assurance from them that if such a program was drawn up and funded they would do their best to make the program work out successfully.

After several weeks of discussion, the Disciple leaders agreed to participate in the program. In the meantime, Rev. Fry and his church staff held meetings with the Ranger leaders. The program ideas were explained to the leaders in detail, and the possibility of a meeting between them and Bernstein was explored.

In one of Bernstein's visits to Chicago, he met with the leadership of both the Rangers and the Disciples. He explained to them in more detail what The Woodlawn Organization was attempting to do, and he pointed out that if both youth organizations participated in a meaningful way there was a possibility that a viable program could be developed. He emphasized, however, repeatedly, that he was in no position to promise that a grant would be forthcoming from OEO. He stated emphatically that he could make no promises. Both the youth groups and The Woodlawn Organization fully understood this.

The Rangers, the Disciples, and TWO appreciated Bernstein's frankness, because none wanted to be the victims of empty promises. During these discussions the gang leadership expressed their desire for what they referred to as a job training program to assist their membership. They stated that time was running out and that they faced an insecure and long, hot summer, with no viable alternative to offer their membership. They expressed their conviction, however, that their membership would not participate in a program that was developed by professionals without any input by the gangs themselves.

The leadership of the two youth organizations met with Bernstein on April 19, 1967 to review the entire proposal and to discuss at length the problems inherent in such a program. They made several constructive suggestions for changes in the program design. Most of these suggestions were incorporated into the proposal.

The gang leadership was informed at this meeting that the probability of obtaining funds for the proposed program was virtually nil as long as the feud between the two gangs continued; that the shootings, killings, and other forms of violence would have to cease if the proposal was to be given consideration by OEO. They were also informed that responsible officials might be skeptical of the sincerity and motives of the two groups who were participating in the proposed program, but that an immediate and complete end to the violence would be tangible evidence of their sincerity. The possibility of a truce between the two youth organizations was discussed.

The following truce between the two youth organizations was signed on April 22 in the office of TWO:

> Date: April 22, 1967
> Time: 12:50 p.m.
> Place: The Woodlawn Organization
> Subject: Understanding between the Disciples and the Blackstone Rangers
>
> This meeting was requested so that there may be some sort of understanding between the leadership of the two abovementioned groups.
>
> There is no treaty, but the two groups have come to an understanding that there will be no weapons used in fighting from here on. But it is understood that if shots are fired between either group, it will endanger the total manpower proposal which was talked about at the recent meeting. The meeting was revolved around the renigade groups running around committing themselves.
>
> In conclusion, if there are any personal problems that you are having with the Rangers and Disciples, please bring it up at meeting and the leaders will try to work it out with you and the party concerned.

There was no evidence of violence between the two organizations after the truce was signed, until well along in the project. Commander Griffin of the Chicago Police Department confirmed that there was a marked drop in violent activity between the gangs after the April 22 meeting.

In summary, the youth organizations endeavored in several dramatic ways to indicate both the critical nature of the needs of the youth of Woodlawn and their conviction that a job training program was the best mechanism to meet those needs. In addition, they gave several tangible indications of their seriousness of intent and willingness to cooperate in a program of which the stated objective was to set up a project that would involve the youth organizations in positive preparation for responsible living.

Chapter Eight

Youth Demonstration Project

The gangs realized that they were expected to break up their gang structure if they expected to participate in traditional agency youth programs. They actively resisted such programs or simply refused to participate. The TWO Project, however, held that (1) it was possible to attain the program objective (gainful employment for participants) without breaking up the gang structure, and (2) the gang structure should be used as a mechanism for involving members of the gangs in the program and for successfully implementing the program.

The Woodlawn Organization believed that by involving the leadership of the two youth organizations in the planning and design of the proposed program, the two organizations would come to identify with it as their own program. Through participation in the development of the program, the organization's leadership would have a stake in its success in terms of ego factors, as well as in terms of jobs that would result from the program. The youth organizational leadership would have a tangible reason for involving their membership in the program. Further, the youth leaders provided the best possible salesmen of the program to the youth of Woodlawn.

In effect, TWO made a "deal" with the two youth organizations, wherein TWO said in effect, "You say you don't want to have anything to do with a program you didn't help to plan. TWO will give you a role in the planning and development of a job training program for the youth of Woodlawn. If you help sell it and make it work, we'll do our best to get it funded and to run the program." The youth leadership did in fact participate in the planning of the proposed program, and took an official position in support of the program.

Use of Gang Members as Subprofessional Staff

TWO used selected gang members as staff persons in the program, thereby making it more acceptable to the gangs. They served as recruiters, basic education instructors, instructor aides, vocational instructor aides, and assistants to the basic education supervisors. Developments in the field of programed instruction made it possible for noncertified, non-college-trained individuals to use programed instructional material with excellent results. The involvement of the indigenous young adults in subprofessional staff positions also provided much-needed immediate employment for a number of persons in the community. TWO used selective criteria to choose the indigenous persons to fill staff positions. Each individual was matched against a detailed job description for each staff slot. Further, the program provided for an initial intensive training and supervision for all indigenous staff members.

Program Policy Board

TWO established a ten-member program policy board, including designated representatives of the youth organizations and adult members of the Woodlawn community at large, with unofficial participation by TWO's staff and the project director. The purpose of the board was to advise TWO on program policy, changes necessary in program design, and selection and review of personnel. The board also purposed to recommend solutions to problems that might arise both within and outside the program, and most important, to maintain clear and regular channels of communication among TWO, the program, the gangs, and the Woodlawn community at large.

The proposed program recognized the wide range of employability among members of the target population. The program came into contact with persons whose work and basic educational skills were so low that they required in-depth training in basic education skills, vocational skills, work orientation, and work attitudes. About 25 percent of the youth recruited by the program had some adaptable work history. Although they did not require great depth or length of training, they were still considered unemployable because they could not obtain and retain jobs.

The training program was therefore originally structured into two tracks. Track one was designed primarily for those who had some sort of work experience, whose literacy and mathematics skills, work orientation, and vocational training. It was intended to work. Track one consisted of a quick brushup of basic education skills, work orientation, and vocational training. It was intended to extend from one to ten weeks. When the staff of the program judged the individuals to be ready for employment, they were to be referred to a job. Track two was specifically designed for the more severely disadvantaged person who had little or no work experience, whose education skills were below the eighth-grade level, whose motivation was low, and who needed extensive vocational training. Track two provided an extensive work orientation and counseling as required. An individual remained in track two for a period of from ten to fifty weeks. When the training program became operational, however, the program was forced to drop track one altogether. The youth who had dropped out of high school were very handicapped educationally. Hardly any were found to be functioning on the eighth-grade level, so all went into track two level.

Recruitment and Intake

Four program centers were established. A subprofessional person recruited youth for the program in the center to which he was assigned. Recruitment, in the main, was conducted by personal contact within the gang structures, and by word of mouth through the same natural communication network. Each center determined the recruitment quota on the basis of the number of training slots open at any given time. If a center had only three slots available only three persons were recruited for that center. The low frustration tolerance of ghetto youth suggested that it would be unwise to accrue a waiting list in excess of five prospective participants. It was essential that the program make no promises, direct or indirect, to the youth of the community that it could not fulfil. Recruitment quotas were therefore strictly observed.

The intake process as well as the vocational assessment took place during the first day the new recruit had contact with the program. This immediate action underscored the reality of the program and kept in check the frustrations that delays and red tape build up in ghetto youth, which might have kept the new recruit from participating in the program.

Vocational Assessment

TWO found that dropout rates could be reduced sharply by placing the new recruit in program services within a day of application. Although the initial vocational assessment was tentative, review of the performance of the recruit in the training components of the program, periodic interviews, and possible retesting provided a flexible situation where he continued to be evaluated in terms of his aptitudes, interests, and performance. Changes in his vocational plan were possible at all points of the training.

The assessment process, under the supervision of professional staff, involved group testing, vocational-interest measurements, and interviews. A great amount of emphasis, however, was placed on the person's past job experience, his vocational interests, and his basic educational skills. The supervisor drew up a plan that included the needs of the individual and an assessment of his personal problems that might interfere with performance in the program and on the job.

Prevocational Training

Some young men needed basic education in addition to job training. Basic education focused on producing functional skills in reading, writing, and mathematics. This component was designed for trainees whose functional literacy and/or mathematics skills fell below the eighth-grade level. Basic education focused on cultivating those skills relevant to obtaining employment and functioning well on the job.

Standardized reading tests were used in this process; but the trainee also learned to fill out typical employment applications and social security forms, and to read job-related instructions typical of those he would encounter in a job situation.

Research has indicated the feasibility of using carefully selected and trained indigenous subprofessional instructors in the classroom. Recent studies have indicated that subprofessional instructors using programed instructional materials can cope with a normal range of problems with a culturally alienated minority group.[1] Basic literacy and basic mathematics classes were therefore staffed by one subprofessional instructor and one subprofessional assistant.

All classes used programed instructional materials. TWO looked for programed materials that were effective in teaching a given skill, had vocationally oriented content, were easily handled by subprofessional instructors, required a minimum of supplementary material and equipment, had a high intrinsic interest for the trainee, and were economical. Staff supervisors made adaptations in the materials and reviewed new materials.

Since no definitive data exist on the effectiveness of such programed literacy and mathematics materials or on the effectiveness of indigenous subprofessional instructors with the proposed target population, efforts were made to conduct the basic-education instruction under quasi-experimental conditions. All trainees were tested prior to beginning the instruction and at interim points, and again at the end of basic-education training, to measure reading and mathematics gains.

Trainees who had functional or near functional reading and mathematics skills were placed in classes called Accelerated Education Review. They needed a brushup review of some literacy and math skills, particularly as they applied in a job context. Class size was held to a maximum of fifteen whenever possible and each class was manned by one subprofessional aide. The instruction lasted up to five hours per day.

Vocational Training

All trainees received work-orientation training. This training aimed primarily at solving the problems of low motivation, nega-

---

[1]Field Test and Evaluation of Four Adult Basic Education Systems conducted by Greenleigh Associates, Inc., Community Action Program, Office of Economic Opportunity, Washington, D.C., 1967, p. 14.

tive attitudes toward work, lack of a concept of the meaning of work, and lack of knowledge of what would be expected of the individual on the job; it also provided a review of the problems the trainee was likely to encounter on the job, and techniques the trainee could use to deal successfully with those problems.

Many trainees had no work experience, while others had negative work experiences. A ghetto youth often does not understand the meaning of employment, its relationship to him and his family, the concept of his responsibility to the employer, the employer's responsibility toward him, the impact regular employment will have on his life, and the adjustments he must make as a result of his employment. The work-orientation training focused on inculcating a functional concept of a job and employment, interpreting the significance of these activities to him, presenting alternative ways for him to deal with this new concept, and anticipating the problems that might arise out of it.

Job Development

TWO consulted with the Illinois Employment Service and other manpower-related agencies and programs to ascertain the job-demand areas in and around Chicago. A partial listing of verified job-demand areas was provided to participants in the program. To assure job availability after training TWO reviewed the job areas, along with new data on job demand during the first month after the project was funded, before finally determining what vocational training the project was to offer.

Job development was a most critical component. Without jobs the program could have only limited effectiveness. Many employers, although they needed personnel, were reluctant to hire the program's trainees because of the notoriety the Woodlawn area, its youth, and its gangs had received over the years on account of violences and a sensational press. TWO and the Chicago Urban League faced the problem of convincing employers to offer jobs and on-the-job training to program participants.

TWO asked the Chicago Urban League to conduct the job-development component of the program. They were skilled in performing job-development activities and had conducted successful on-the-job training programs.

Follow-up Services

The period covering the first six weeks to two months after the graduate from the program begins employment, according to other manpower research, is the most critical for the individual in terms of his making lasting adjustment to the job and to the new life pattern that results from his employment. TWO believed that extensive follow-up services had to be an integral part of the total program of service. Follow-up on all program graduates who entered employment was carried out by the staff member who initially recruited the individual for the program, or by the supportive-services supervisor along with the Chicago Urban League.

Supportive Services

A number of supportive services were provided by the project. These included continuing personal contact from the recruiter, the classroom instructor, and staff personnel. The primary adviser was the recruiter. This program offered a chance to evaluate the feasibility of using subprofessional persons for this counseling support rather than using a professional counselor. The supportive relationship was effective in assisting the trainee to make the necessary growth and adjustment to himself, the training program, and the job.

Stipends

TWO paid all persons enrolled in the program a training stipend, which was a form of scholarship. Weekly stipends were $45 per week, contingent on attendance in the classes. Deductions were made if the trainee skipped classes.

Traditional job training programs frequently operate on the assumption that the trainee must "learn" to respond in a manner consistent with values of middle-class culture and that he must learn to do so within the first few weeks of the program. One of these values is to postpone immediate satisfaction in favor of long-range goals. Such projects often fail to recognize the alienated ghetto youth's inability to perceive or to place value in long-range goals, or to invest himself in a situation that provides no immediate reward in the interest of longer-range benefits. The youth's demand for immediate results is often viewed as psychopathy, "lack of motivation," a "behavior problem," or the like. The ghetto youth, however, usually cannot perceive long-range goals simply because he has never reaped any long-range benefit from any activity he has ever engaged in—school, interpersonal relationships, employment. Moreover, if he has ever experienced a long-range by-product from any of his actions, it was likely to have been negative—confinement in an institution, prolonged poverty, hunger, frequent encounters with the police. He is forced to live for today with little concern for tomorrow, for if tomorrow comes it offers him only more uncertainty. He usually tries to "beat the system" and approaches most institutions and most people as part of the system he has to beat. This is not only what the social scientist may call his "orientation," it is a life style for survival both within the ghetto and in the world beyond.

It is at least as unrealistic to expect such youth to adjust to another standard and to develop longer-range goals in a relatively short period of time, as it is for the professional social worker to learn to respond only in terms of the immediate situation while disregarding long-range consequences. Ghetto youth cannot make such an adaptation, certainly not in a short period of time. Further, there is real question whether or not the values and orientation of these youth are any less valid for them than middle-class standards.

TWO believes that ghetto youth can learn to adjust to the society at large by learning how to utilize their existing life style in a more functional manner, and that in so doing they can gradually learn new patterns of performance and interaction.

The project paid cash incentives to staff members, based on a relatively long-range assessment of the value of the individual staff members' performance on the job. TWO paid a five-dollar bonus to all recruitment/follow-up staff members for each person they recruited into track two who remained in the program on a full time basis (with less than 10 percent absences) for a minimum of five weeks. Further, they were paid a five-dollar bonus for each person to whom they provided follow-up services who remained on the job (either on-the-job training or on a permanent job) on a full-time basis (with less than 10 percent absences) for a minimum period of six weeks. TWO paid a five-dollar bonus to the indigenous prevocational training staff on the basis of the effectiveness of their instruction of trainees assigned to their classes.

The payment of bonuses was dependent solely on performance measurements both of the subprofessional staff member and of the trainees for whom he was responsible. Professional supervisory staff maintained all performance records and made all relevant evaluations to obtain such performance data. The professional supervisory personnel were responsible for issuing periodic performance evaluations to all indigenous staff to keep them abreast of their relative performance in the program. There were some obvious pitfalls to this incentive system.

In-Service Training

The project director was to assume responsibility for in-depth and in-service training programs for all subprofessional staff. However, a project director was never appointed. The initial in-service training that subprofessional staff members received spanned a period of two to four weeks and was initiated during the first month of the program. The training included an analysis of the objectives of the program, techniques used in attaining those objectives, specific responsibilities of all staff, lines of authority and communication, program policies as they apply to the staff and to trainees, techniques of literacy training, math training, vocational training, formal counseling.

The supervisory personnel conducted in-service training periodically throughout the project. The supervisory staff also evaluated the performance of all subprofessional staff members and submitted monthly evaluation reports.

Chapter Nine

Death of the Youth Demonstration Project

The Youth Demonstration Project had two lives. The first was its internal life, the training of young people within the Woodlawn community to become productive, self-determined members of society. The second life was the larger life of the project within the System—how it was related to the political, economic, and social life not only of Chicago, but of the nation. It was this System that refused to sustain the life of the project and finally succeeded in killing it. Even a member of the white Establishment suffered professionally because of the support he gave to the project. This chapter will describe the means by which the System harassed the project to death.

In early 1967, TWO notified Dr. Deton Brooks, Executive Director of the Chicago Committee on Urban Opportunity (CCUO), that The Woodlawn Organization was drawing up a proposal to be submitted to the Office of Economic Opportunity (OEO) that would involve the Blackstone Rangers and the Eastside Disciples in a basic-education job training program, and asked for his support. At that time, Dr. Brooks indicated that he was pleased about this kind of program and stated that he would be very happy to see as much poverty money coming into Chicago as was possible.

The Chicago Committee on Urban Opportunity handles all the federal money that comes into Chicago for poverty programs. This is a sizeable sum of money totaling many millions of dollars. Brooks was appointed executive director of CCUO by Mayor Daley and was responsible directly to the mayor.

As stated earlier, one source of power is money. The mayor through CCUO, therefore, exerted a great deal of power over the poverty-stricken people of Chicago. To state the matter in terms all black people understand, the white Establishment, as represented by the mayor's office, had the power of life and death over one of the poor's main sources of hope—financial aid from the federal government. The OEO money funneled through Brooks' office gave city hall a tremendously powerful hold on black people through the patronage that such money made possible.

TWO also contacted John Root of the Metropolitan YMCA hoping that the YMCA would participate in the project by taking over the on-the-job training component of the project.

Although Root and Brooks seemed to be highly favorable toward what TWO was doing in the beginning, as the weeks wore on and negotiations between TWO and OEO began to bear fruit, both men began to cool to the idea of a Youth Demonstration Project.

Every alarm system in the white Establishment in Chicago flashed red and clanged loudly at the prospect of Woodlawn's obtaining funding by its own efforts, for its own project, without the aid or approval of the powers that be. From the moment Brooks correctly perceived TWO's position relative to this grant, CCUO began to work actively to defeat the project. Brooks argued that any program of this magnitude should be funded through the local office, not directly from Washington. In this he had considerable cooperation from Mr. Root of the YMCA. After the program was funded, Root's position shifted, and he became somewhat in support of the project. CCUO, however, remained an implacable enemy of the project to its end.

Not only was Brooks opposed to it, but so also were others of the mayor's advisers and some of the city agencies that dealt with youth problems, such as the Chicago Youth Commission. These agencies, although they had not been able to carry out a program for youth that would end the violence and strife that were constantly erupting between the two gangs, were unalterably opposed to having the OEO fund The Woodlawn Organization's program.

Almost all the mayor's advisers were against the proposal. In view of this opposition the mayor did not commit himself in favor of the program at that time. At a later date, however, the mayor did commit himself. This affirmative commitment was made in his office in a meeting attended by Julian Levi of the University of Chicago, Edwin C. Berry, executive director of the Chicago Urban League, a businessman in the Woodlawn community, and the president of TWO. The mayor's chief concern seemed to be that the program should not be limited to gang members only, and when TWO agreed to open the project to nonmembers he said the project was acceptable to him. The mayor's advisers, however, continued to be opposed to the project.

In spite of this opposition Jerome Bernstein, deputy director of the manpower division of the Community Action Programs section of the OEO, continued to press for funding of TWO's proposal for a demonstration youth project. It is entirely possible that it was Bernstein's consistent and unswerving support of TWO that eventually cost him his job.

Bernstein's superior, Donald Hess, came to Chicago to iron out the difficulties. He met with Dr. Brooks, representing the CCUO, and Alan Beales, regional director of OEO. The TWO president had expected to meet with them, representing TWO. He was specifically asked, however, not to attend this meeting. It was behind closed doors that Hess, Beales, and Brooks hammered out a set of special conditions on which the funding of this grant was contingent.

After the meeting Hess disclosed to TWO what the special conditions were and indicated that this was the best OEO could do. If TWO wanted the program, they would have to submit to the special conditions that had been agreed upon in Beales' office. It was only with the greatest reluctance and apprehension that TWO agreed to the special conditions, and only because there was no way to oppose the Establishment in this matter.

There were fifteen special conditions in the agreement, most of which were acceptable to TWO. Four were objectionable to TWO and one of these four gave the mayor's office a stranglehold on the project—concurrence in the selection of the project director. These four were as follows.

1. In view of the importance of this demonstration to the City of Chicago, the Office of the Mayor of the City of Chicago

shall be invited to concur in the Grantee's selection of the Project Director.

2. The Grantee shall initiate negotiations with CCUO for the provision of all legal services required by the project, including the provision of legal services to project participants. . . .
3. The Grantee shall negotiate a contract with CCUO for the provision of bookkeeping services to the project. . . .
4. CCUO may, at its discretion, request through the Office of Program Planning, CAP/OEO, to participate in monitoring and evaluating activities with regard to the fiscal and programmatic conduct of the project. . . . It is understood by the Grantee, CCUO and OEO that any OEO approved monitoring or evaluation activities carried out independently by CCUO will not constitute or result in any control of the project by CCUO. . . .

Concurrence of the mayor in selection of the project director seems innocent enough, and is the kind of condition most whites would consider entirely reasonable. In fact, white people become extremely uneasy whenever control of a project slips out of their hands and into the hands of black people. Everyone in the black community, however, is painfully aware that a favorite and almost universally successful tactic of the white Establishment for keeping blacks in line is to control black leadership, either by buying it off or by controlling who the black leaders will be. The special conditions attached to this project gave the mayor's office precisely that power.

It is worthy of note that subsequent to the funding of the grant, city hall denied that it was a party to the formulation of the special conditions. After the meeting between Brooks, Hess, and Beales, Brooks agreed to the special conditions as laid down and agreed that the city would cooperate with the program if these special conditions were followed.

The program was funded by OEO on May 31, 1967, and the total federal funds awarded were $927,341. This program was to run for one year.

Under the law governing research and demonstration grants funded by OEO, the governor of any state must approve. On June 19, 1967, Governor Otto Kerner in a letter to Theodore Berry, director of the Community Action Programs of OEO, gave his consent to the grant for TWO's youth project.

TWO immediately started implementing the newly funded program. The president contacted Edward Elwin of New York, who had been highly recommended for the position of project director. TWO met with Elwin, discussed the project with him, and invited him to come to Chicago to meet with the youth leaders. Elwin agreed to come, and his meeting with the youth leaders was satisfactory. They seemed to understand him and he seemed to get along well with them.

Elwin's credentials for the job of project director were impeccable. He was a registered psychologist in the state of New York as well as a registered social worker. He had received his AB from Brooklyn College and his MA in clinical psychology from New York University. He also received an MA in correctional administration, a form of public administration. He was a doctoral candidate at New York University in social psychology.

Elwin's job record included supervisor of the probation department of the Supreme Court's Second Judicial Court of New York. He had been consultant to the President's District of Columbia Crime Commission and to the American Correctional Association. He had the sole responsibility for study and evaluation of the probation system in the District of Columbia. The report, which was concluded and given to the President of the United States on September 15, 1966, proposed major modifications of the probation system, calling for utilization of anti-poverty and community action programs in the treatment of delinquents and the dismissal of indictments for first offenders who had successfully completed probation.

He had also taught criminology at the graduate level, worked for the New York State Division of Parole in New York City, and helped create and later evaluate the structure of the governor's program for specialized intensive treatment of parolees who had been drug addicts in New York.

TWO offered Elwin the job of project director, and he agreed to leave his position in New York and come to Chicago to take up this new position if the mayor would concur in his slection. TWO was confident that the mayor of Chicago would have no problem in concurring in the selection of a man with such a background.

The Woodlawn Organization project needed the most experienced man available. Never for a moment did TWO think that Mayor Daley would reject a man with such impressive credentials.

The mayor's office, however, would not concur in the appointment of Mr. Elwin as project director. After several unsatisfactory meetings with the mayor and with Dr. Brooks, TWO set up a blue-ribbon advisory committee to review all candidates for the position, including the two men recommended by Brooks.[1] Brooks was invited to serve on this committee, since he was executive director of CCUO and the program was of great importance to the city of Chicago; but he refused.

In a later meeting between Brooks and TWO's president, called at Brooks' request, TWO again invited him to participate. He was extremely negative, however, and said that the TWO advisory committee was incompetent and knew nothing about poverty, the poor, or Woodlawn.

Brooks was asked for the names of the two men he had recommended to the OEO in Washington for the position of project director. They were Alfred Pritchard and John Carter Ford. TWO wanted them to go before the advisory committee along with Elwin. TWO agreed to let the advisory committee make its recommendation to the mayor.

Brooks steadfastly refused to allow the two men he had recommended to appear before this committee. TWO, however, invited them by letter, as follows:

> Your name has been submitted to the Office of Economic Opportunity in Washington, D.C. as a possible candidate for the

[1] Members of the advisory committee were: Dr. Irving Stergel, Professor, School of Social Service, University of Chicago; Dr. Robert Hess, Chairman, Committee on Human Development, University of Chicago; Dr. Julian Levi, Executive Director, Southeast Chicago Commission; Edward Berry, Executive Director, Chicago Urban League; Harry Cain, National Institutes of Mental Health, Washington, D.C.; Richard Boone, Executive Director, Citizens Crusade Against Poverty, Washington, D.C.; Sheppard Kellum, Psychiatrist, Woodlawn Mental Health Center; Willem Richelen Hendrik Smit, Manager, Community Development Operations, Xerox Educational Division, New York; Dr. June Tapp, Psychologist, University of Chicago. There were also two representatives of TWO. Mr. Smit later resigned from the committee because TWO signed a contract with Xerox to provide curricular materials for the program. Dr. Spergel also resigned because he was engaged by OEO to evaluate the program.

> position of Project Director for the total Manpower Program for 700 out-of-school, unemployed youth, which is a demonstration program operated by The Woodlawn Organization. . . . To assure the selection of the most qualified individuals for staff positions in this demonstration project, The Woodlawn Organization has established an Advisory Committee of prominent professionals of both National and Local stature. It will be the function of this committee to review all applicants for the position of Project Director. . . . You are invited to attend a meeting of the subcommittee of this Advisory Committee on Thursday, August 3, at 7:30 p.m.

A few days later TWO received from each of the two men a telegram stating: "I respectfully decline to attend the advisory sub-committee meeting on August 3, 1967, at 7:30 p.m. The conditions expressed in the letter are unacceptable to me at this time."

TWO was never able to understand what conditions were unacceptable to the men, because there were no conditions stated in the letter. Elwin, however, having received the same kind of letter as that sent to Brooks' nominees, flew to Chicago from New York and met with the subcommittee of the advisory committee.

After a long interview with Elwin and after close examination of the resumes of the other two men, the subcommittee unanimously voted to recommend Elwin as the most qualified candidate for the office of project director.

The mayor's office again rejected Elwin, however, because he did not live in Chicago. The mayor said he felt that surely in Chicago there must be someone who would qualify for the position of project director.[2]

The Woodlawn Organization immediately began to search for another candidate. They found a suitable candidate in Ashby Smith, who was at that time working in a supervisory capacity with the Chicago Urban League.

A meeting was held with the mayor, Ashby Smith, Brooks, and TWO's president. The mayor seemed satisfied with Smith's credentials. He then asked Smith the key question: Would he as project

---

[2] It is interesting to note that after the police scandal in Chicago several years ago, the mayor did not restrict his efforts to find a new police chief merely to the city of Chicago but looked over the entire nation, and finally hired Orlando Wilson from California.

director bring the TWO program under the total comprehensive control of CCUO? The TWO president indicated to the mayor that Smith did not have the authority to bring the project under the direction and direct control of Brooks; that this was a demonstration project funded directly out of Washington to The Woodlawn Organization as grantee, and any such decision would have to be made with The Woodlawn Organization; that neither the president of TWO nor Ashby Smith had the authority to say that he would bring the program under the control of CCUO. With that the mayor withheld his concurrence in appointment of Ashby Smith. It later became evident that the mayor's office would not concur on anybody The Woodlawn Organization appointed unless he had ironclad assurances that the program would be brought under the control of the city agency.

During this time The Woodlawn Organization was seeking to implement the youth demonstration program. TWO had been told by OEO that Brooks had agreed on the special conditions. TWO entered into this project in good faith expecting some cooperation from CCUO and other Chicago agencies.

It soon became clear, however, that even though Brooks had participated with Alan Beales and Donald Hess in the drawing up of the special conditions, TWO could expect no cooperation whatsoever in the operation of this manpower program for gang youth in Woodlawn.

The mayor's office would not have been able to obstruct the work of the youth development project without tacit support from the white community, based on the traditional assumption that black people are incapable of handling their own affairs.

Police Harassment

The project was no sooner funded that it ran into difficulty with the gang intelligence unit (GIU) of the Chicago Police Department. On June 6, 1967, The Woodlawn Organization called a meeting of the leaders of the Blackstone Rangers and the Eastside Disciples to explain to them the special conditions of the grant and exactly how the program would operate. All the youth leaders attended the meeting.

Other persons present were Leon Finney, staff director of TWO,

Jerome Bernstein of OEO, and members of the TWO staff who were employed in TWO projects unrelated to the youth project. The TWO president was there also.

The meeting was progressing in an orderly fashion. At approximately 2:15 p.m., officers of the GIU pulled up and parked in front of TWO's office. The officers surveyed the premises for approximately fifteen minutes. The gang youths responded to this surveillance by requesting to meet in the inner offices of TWO. After the gang youths had moved into the inner offices, the GIU officers invaded the premises of TWO. At this point, the youths attempted to leave the premises peacefully.

During the interim, approximately six regular squad cars, two policemen in each, and six more gang intelligence officers formed a barricade to prevent the egress of the gang youths. The GIU officer who was in charge of the barricade stated that he was going to arrest everyone on the premises of TWO, including the professional staff.

Leon Finney, staff director of TWO, contacted Commander William B. Griffin of the third district and informed him of the near crisis situation that had evolved. Commander Griffin responded by saying that apparently not all of the policemen at the site of The Woodlawn Organization were under his command. He indicated, however, that since the meeting was a peaceful one and no laws had been violated, he would send a field lieutenant out to disperse the uniformed officers. He then suggested that the head of the city-wide GIU be contacted. Finney did so immediately and was told by the chief that he understood the situation as it was described to him and asked that TWO bear with the police until Lt. Buckney of the GIU arrived to disperse the GIU officers.

At approximately 2:45 p.m. a lieutenant of the third district uniformed police and Lt. Buckney of GIU arrived at the scene. The lieutenant from the third district immediately moved to disperse the uniformed policemen. Lt. Buckney approached Leon Finney and requested full details as to what had transpired. After Finney explained what had happened, Lt. Buckney said, "Let's have a compromise; we will let all of the gang youth go if we can have the names of everyone present at this meeting." Finney told Lt. Buckney that his compromise was unthinkable, that TWO was holding a peaceful meeting, that there was no disturbance, no one had made any complaints, that everyone's civil rights were being violated and that the police were exceeding their authority.

Finney again contacted downtown headquarters to explain the newly evolved situation. The chief of the gang intelligence unit immediately saw the injustice and asked to speak to Lt. Buckney. Apparently Lt. Buckney was countermanded, for shortly thereafter all policemen were dispersed from the premises and from the immediate vicinity of the TWO office, and all the youth leaders were allowed to leave the premises peacefully.

Ironically, this very police raid probably saved the youth project. The youth were very much disturbed about the special conditions of the grant, which seemed to involve the police department and the Chicago Committee on Urban Opportunity to a great degree. This, coupled with a recent newspaper article in the *Chicago Daily News* stating that The Woodlawn Organization had apparently made a deal with the mayor's office, aroused the suspicions of the youth leaders. The suspicion among the youth was so great that the discussions were about to break down. They said they would have nothing to do with the program, and were ready to leave; at that moment the police barged in and prevented them from leaving. The young men understood right then that TWO was not in league with city hall or the police department. After the incident was closed, the youth agreed to work with the program. The very program that the GIU despised and city hall did not want would have died aborning had it not been for the bungling of the gang intelligence unit.

The problems with the police declined in frequency after the project got into full swing. By the middle of the summer of 1967, the gang problems diminished to such a degree that the president of TWO was able to write the following letter to Jerome Bernstein. In view of the incident reported next in this chapter, however, the letter takes on prophetic proportions.

> DEAR MR. BERNSTEIN:
> As of this date we have had no further problems with the Police Department as we endeavor to implement our program.
> However, I do have some fears that I would like to relate to you. My experience with the Police Department has been of a limited nature, and while I have read newspaper accounts of persons accusing policemen of planting illegal articles in order to justify

arrests, I have always taken these charges with a grain of salt. In view of the clearly illegal action taken by the police in the June 6th incident at The Woodlawn Organization, I am now inclined to give more credence to the above mentioned newspaper reports.

We are fully cognizant of the character of the target population of our program and have no desire to interfere with or impede normal police activity; and while I am sure that the Police Department does not condone nor approve the kind of activity relating to the charges that have been reported by the newspapers, it is always possible that some overzealous policeman might get "carried away" in his efforts to perform his duty.

This is a fear we have and I am relating it to you.

The Spread of Harassment

It soon became clear not only that the project was to be subjected to the harassment of the police, but that even a member of the Establishment, Jerome Bernstein, was to feel the political sting of city hall as a result of his association with and support of the TWO youth project.

The incident that became the catalyst for Bernstein's eventual dismissal was an episode revolving around a meeting that he set up between a group of people from the Watts district in Los Angeles and the Rangers. The circumstances that led up to the meeting are as follows: In July 1967, TWO contacted Bernstein, who was the project manager,[3] with respect to the considerable friction between the Eastside Disciples and the Blackstone Rangers. This friction came about primarily over an incident on Saturday, July 22, when a hundred Rangers marched through Woodlawn over the turf of the Disciples: this was tantamount to a declaration of war. It was reported that they had beaten up a member of the Eastside Disciples. This incident along with an argument between two of the rival leaders on another occasion appeared to be a breakdown in Ranger-Disciple cooperation. Furthermore, it became difficult to keep up with fast-moving events, and TWO indicated to Bernstein that the situation was in danger of getting completely out of control. Detroit had already erupted and serious rioting was in

[3] The project manager must be distinguished from the project director. The project manager is an OEO person in charge of the project but based in Washington.

progress there. There were wild rumors circulating all over Chicago that Chicago was due to erupt any minute.

On Monday, July 24, rumors were circulating throughout the Woodlawn community that Woodlawn would be burned that evening. Many businesses closed down early Monday afternoon in expectation of violence. After consultation the TWO staff came to the conclusion that (1) there was the possibility of an attack on the Rangers by the Disciples to even the score resulting from the Rangers' Saturday march into Disciple territory; (2) such an event, coupled with the rapidly spreading rumors about riots, could touch off a wider-scale conflict, possibly even a full-scale riot throughout the city; (3) conditions of hysteria on both the west side and south side were growing worse by the hour, and almost any incident could trigger a riot. These views were shared by other people consulted by TWO. In short, many parties in Chicago were convinced that an outbreak of riots in Woodlawn was imminent. For these reasons the TWO president contacted Jerome Bernstein.

Bernstein came to Chicago immediately. He related that several of the leaders of the Blackstone Rangers had at some prior time visited the Watts area in Los Angeles for the purpose of seeing how the Watts ghetto had organized itself. According to Bernstein, a mutuality of respect developed between the Rangers and some of the Watts people during the visit.

In view of the gravity of the situation and TWO's extreme concern with respect to an imminent outbreak of hostilities between the Rangers and Disciples, Bernstein suggested that TWO send for a group of the Watts people to come to Chicago to talk with some of the leaders of the youth groups. TWO consented to do this. Bernstein and the TWO president agreed that any such meeting should be held downtown rather than in the Woodlawn neighborhood. It was their belief that if such a meeting were held in Woodlawn TWO would run the risk of being accused of bringing in outsiders to foment a riot.

Bernstein then contacted the Watts group and they flew into Chicago. They met with Bernstein and some of the Ranger leaders the same night. TWO personnel never met the Watts people, nor did they participate in the meeting. Bernstein, however, communicated the essence of the meeting, which was that the participants spoke of the brotherhood of black people, the need for them to join together for their own good, and their need to make decisions for their own community, and urged that a riot would produce nothing positive for them. The meeting was a success. The next day the leaders of both Woodlawn youth groups came into the TWO office and stated that there would be no gang war and that they would do everything they could to keep riots out of Woodlawn.

They were true to their word. Although there were sporadic incidents between individual members of both groups, there was no gang war; and the youth worked diligently to prevent rioting in Woodlawn, both in the summer of 1967 and again in the spring of 1968 when Martin Luther King was assassinated. Chicago's west side erupted shortly after King's assassination. Large areas on the west side were put to the torch and nine people were killed. The situation got completely out of control of the local authorities and the National Guard was called in.

During the period, the members of the Eastside Disciples and the Blackstone Rangers met at a major intersection, 63rd street and Woodlawn Avenue. They numbered about four thousand youth altogether. The purpose of the meeting was to work out a method whereby they could help prevent rioting in their community. The meeting was successful. There were no riots in Woodlawn. The meeting between the Watts group and the Ranger leadership had evidently borne fruit far beyond anything TWO had imagined.

There was, however, one unfortunate occurrence that grew out of the meeting. The Watts people were arrested by the police and Bernstein himself was detained and questioned at length. The Watts group had been arrested in their hotel room and some marijuana and a gun were found allegedly in their possession. After extensive questioning, however, they were all released and they then returned to Los Angeles. There was a tremendous effort on the part of the police and city hall to make it appear that the Watts people were brought in to cause trouble and that Bernstein was the instigator of it all. They could never substantiate the charge, however, because the exact opposite occurred. There was no trouble. In fact, their trip made a direct contribution to the peace of Woodlawn. Not long afterward, Bernstein was dismissed from OEO.

In the meantime, TWO continued to spend the entire summer preparing for the classes that were scheduled to open in September.

During the summer, both the Rangers and the Disciples worked hard in a successful effort to keep violence out of Woodlawn. An example of their efforts in keeping Woodlawn cool can be seen in an incident that occurred July 31, 1967, in which a black man was shot and killed. The alleged assailant was a white store-owner. The *Chicago Sun Times* covered the incident and wrote the following story:

> TWO YOUTH GANGS HAILED FOR PEACE ROLE
>
> by Lillian Calhoun and
> Christopher Chandler
>
> Youth gangs in the South Side community of Woodlawn were credited Thursday with playing a key role in quelling what might have been a serious outbreak of violence earlier this week.
>
> The Disciples and the Blackstone Rangers helped restore calm to their neighborhood Tuesday after a shooting near 67th and Cottage Grove threatened to erupt into a major incident, observers said.
>
> Praise for the work of the youth gang members came from Deputy Police Chief Samuel W. Nolan, newly named head of the department's community services division; Edwin C. Berry, executive director of the Chicago Urban League, and the Rev. Arthur M. Brazier, president of The Woodlawn Organization.
>
> All three men agreed that the cooperation of the gangs and swift police action in arresting the white store-owner who fatally wounded a Negro, were the major factors in restoring calm to the area.

William Griffin, police commander of the third district, also indicated that the youths were helpful in maintaining peace. In a letter to TWO dealing with related subjects, he stated that the youths were very helpful in maintaining peace within the community following the shooting incident.

On August 2, 1967 Nick Dorenzo, a leader of the Disciples, and certain of his associates appeared in Commander Griffin's office and made known to him their plans to circulate throughout the community in an effort to maintain peace and report any foreign agitation. These youths were furnished identification by the police commander that would make police officers aware that they were working in accord with the police department.

On September 11, 1967, TWO opened its first classes. Throughout the fall months, TWO continued to operate the program in spite of not having appointed an experienced project director. Within thirty days four training centers opened with over one-hundred youth enrolled. Almost immediately, gang intelligence unit harassment began again. Detectives from GIU would walk into the centers without a warrant and interrogate someone. On occasion, they would take trainees away from the centers. Frequently, detectives would stop trainees on the street as they left the centers, either for lunch or at the end of the training day. The youth repeatedly complained to TWO about the harassment, but TWO was unable to prevent this undue police activity. It appeared to be set policy.

Press Harassment

While the project was harassed throughout the summer and fall, the full attack on the program did not come until winter. On the morning of December 22, 1967, the first blow fell.

The *Chicago Tribune* carried a sensational story with the lead headline reading: *FIVE OEO AIDS FACE KILLING, RAPE TRIALS*. The story began by saying: "At least five members of a southside youth gang, all awaiting trial on charges ranging from murder to rape, have held top administrative and teaching jobs for a $927,000 War on Poverty Program, the Tribune learned yesterday." This story produced sensational news that was carried by the wire services throughout the country.

The story was slanted to put the project in the worst possible light. It did not in any way show that the program was designed to deal with alienated youth, many of whom had been in trouble with the law in the past. The story did not give all of the facts—for instance, it did not say that one of the youths held on murder charges had resigned from the program prior to his arrest, nor did it state that the other youth had been suspended from the program on the day he was arrested.

It is significant that the news story did not break until two months after the arrests were made. As to the youth held on rape charges, TWO's position was that these youth would not be dismissed from the program until they were proven guilty. The youth who were facing rape charges were out on bond while the youth facing murder charges were imprisoned.

The next day, December 23, 1967, the *Tribune* printed another story with the lead headline reading: *DALEY ASSAILS TWO USE OF US CASH*. The article began, "Mayor Daley sharply criticized the $927,000 Federal anti-povery program administered by TWO yesterday, and said no program should be geared to appeal to youth gang members."

There was a demand that TWO fire all the youth who had criminal charges against them. It was TWO's position, however, that the mere presence of charges does not constitute guilt. This position is built on the cornerstone of the justice system in America. Therefore, TWO in a special meeting decided that all youth who were in jail would be suspended from the project; youth charged with crimes but out on bond would remain in the project until proven guilty.

According to the December 23, 1967 issue of the *Sun Times,* Mayor Daley called for the dismissal of antipovery workers employed by the TWO Project if they proved to have serious criminal records. TWO refused to take that kind of action, primarily because the project was specifically designed to reach alienated youth most of whom did have police records of some kind. For three days the controversy raged in the newspaper and on television. On December 24 the *Chicago Tribune* ran another story, the lead headline reading: *OEO STEPS INTO UPROAR OVER T.W.O. FUND USE*. The article read:

> A top antipoverty official vowed yesterday to take immediate steps to correct the situation in which south side gang members with police records or who are awaiting trial are employed in a federally financed program as teachers and administrators. . . . "We will not tolerate destructive elements in this or any other program financed by OEO," Alan Beals, Great Lakes Regional Director for the Office of Economic Opportunity, said. "Moreover," continued Beals, "OEO will take any corrective measures needed to assure that the project will attain its goal in a manner consistent with the public safety, community welfare, and the legal rights of individuals." . . . The Rev. Arthur M. Brazier, TWO president, has indicated he will take no action to remove the gang members until the cases are settled in Court.

The *Chicago Tribune* continued its attack. On December 26 it ran a headline: *QUIT SCHOOL FOR EASY MONEY GANG LEADERS URGE.* On the same date Congressman Roman Pucinski entered the fray. The *Chicago Tribune* stated the following:

> Representative Roman Pucinski, Democratic member of Congress from Illinois said yesterday that the Office of Economic Opportunity in Washington has opened an investigation of program planning and expenditures and that he has asked them to turn the results of the investigations over to the Chicago Committee on Urban Opportunity. . . . Pucinski said he has asked the General Accounting Office in Washington to audit TWO's records and report on the organization's expenditures.

The attacks on the project continued. Whenever any youth who was a member of the project ran afoul of the law, the news was printed in the *Chicago Tribune.* The article would state the facts in the case and then connect the youth to the project, similar to the way newspapers had in the past indicated that a person arrested for a crime was a Negro. This would happen even though the crime with which the youth was charged had no bearing on the project. For instance, in an earlier report, on September 17, 1967, the *Tribune* ran an article about a youth employed in the project who was arrested and charged with a shooting. The headline read: *T.W.O. TEACHER IS CHARGED IN DEATH OF GIRL.* This was the pattern that existed over a period of several months.

The Office of Economic Opportunity sent its investigators to Chicago to look into TWO's operation of the project. Their investigators gave the project a thorough study and found that TWO was not guilty of program mismanagement. At the close of their investigation, TWO received a communication from Theodore Berry, Director of OEO's Community Action Programs. Dated January 27, 1968, it stated: "This project has national significance in testing program mechanisms to serve the hard core poor male young adult. This age group is a great concern of our country both in terms of their human potential and their potential for anti-social behavior. O.E.O. fully supports this program effort you have undertaken."

Backed by the support of OEO, TWO's president called a press conference and issued a statement to all Chicago newspapers and television stations. In his statement he responded to two main criticisms of TWO's youth development project. One criticism was that TWO did not fire all persons associated with the project who were charged with or indicted for serious crimes. TWO's position was that all persons so charged were presumed innocent until proven guilty, and until convicted were to remain on the project if they were released on bond and able to perform their assigned tasks.

The second charge leveled against TWO was that it recruited students by encouraging them to drop out of school. OEO made the following declaration: "Our investigation disclosed one ineligible student in the program. The student had falsely represented his age to project officials. He was dropped from the program several months ago."

TWO's president went on to say that TWO and OEO were in wholehearted agreement that the program should have strong management and high standards of project performance.

One of the results of the continuing press harassment was that OEO, the sponsoring organization of TWO's youth development project, began to respond to the attacks with additional requirements, supposedly to tighten the administration of the project. For the most part, TWO agreed with the new requirements since the project was already performing a large number of them. TWO was able to reach agreement with OEO on the other requirements after TWO's president conferred with OEO officials.

Even though at the end of its investigation the OEO backed The Woodlawn Organization's handling of the project, the *Chicago Tribune* continued to attack TWO, and in addition fired a broadside at OEO. On January 27, 1968, the following headline appeared: *O.E.O. DECLINES TO GET FELONS OFF T.W.O. JOB.* The article began by saying: "The Office of Economic Opportunity (O.E.O.) announced that persons who now have criminal records will be allowed to continue teaching and administrating in the $927,000 poverty program directed by The Woodlawn Organization (T.W.O.)."

Not one of the youth who featured in the sensational murder and rape charges was ever convicted. The newspaper attacks began in December 1967, and as of November 1968, not one of these youth had been brought to trial. In fact, after all the sensational publicity, all the charges were dropped, but by that time incalculable damage had been done to the project and to TWO.

In early January 1968, three men from the General Accounting Offices (GAO) came into TWO's youth project. They stated that they had been instructed by a congressman to audit the financial records of the youth project. When asked what congressman had given them such instructions they politely refused to divulge his name. The TWO president indicated to them that TWO was eager to have the truth known about its fiscal management of the project and would cooperate with them in every way. This team of three men remained at The Woodlawn Organization's offices on a day-to-day basis, from the first part of January until the middle of March. They scrutinized the entire fiscal operation in minute detail. They found that TWO was in no way mismanaging government funds. These findings, so favorable to TWO, were never given newspaper coverage.

The McClellan Hearing

In the meantime, a team from the senate subcommittee on investigations, chaired by Senator John McClellan of Arkansas, set up offices in Chicago and launched an investigation of TWO's youth project. Their investigation continued for several months and culminated in public hearings in Washington.

The hearings occupied the headlines for days, with serious charges being made against Rev. John Fry. The First Presbyterian Church had granted facilities to the Blackstone Rangers for meeting purposes and had become known as the Ranger's headquarters. TWO had also leased some space on the third floor of the huge edifice for use as one of its training centers. Rev. Fry and the First Presbyterian Church had long been a thorn in the side of the gang intelligence unit because of their work with the Ranger organization. The Senate committee dug up two witnesses who leveled sensational charges against Rev. Fry. They were George Rose and Annabelle Martin. Several Chicago policemen backed up the charges. The charges were that guns were stored in the church, that sex orgies were carried on in the church, that Rev. Fry had transmitted an order to have someone killed, that marijuana was packaged and sold on the church premises, and so on. As one would expect, these charges made sensational headlines even though they were denied categorically by Rev. Fry.

Rev. Fry was the victim of a grave injustice. He was never allowed to have witnesses called in to testify on his behalf nor was his lawyer allowed to cross-examine those who were hurling the accusations. The entire hearings were conducted along these lines. Throughout the hearings, Rev. Fry never was given an opportunity adequately to answer the unfounded accusations against him.

Four months later, however, Rev. Fry made a speech at a symposium on the McClellan hearings at the Hyde Park Union Church. This symposium was held under the auspices of the Hyde Park-Kenwood Council of Synagogues and Churches on Sunday, October 20, 1968.

Rev. Fry first pointed out the three options available on encountering the testimony adverse to First Presbyterian Church—(1) accepting all the testimony against the church, the staff, and Rev. Fry himself as true; (2) believing that the three staff members plus the Blackstone Rangers conspired to keep the alleged activities completely secret; (3) realizing that maliciously untrue information was introduced in Washington.

He went on to show how neither of the first two options was valid, and that the third option was held by the session, staff, congregation of First Church, members of TWO, and virtually everyone in Woodlawn. He said:

> This is the only option for us because our experience confirms our innocence of the charges. We need construct no intellectual theory to explain why we are innocent and we need not explain why George Rose, Annabelle Martin, and assorted policemen said what they did.
>
> We do not even consider this an option. We consider it the lived truth of our common life. We knew of no marijuana use, distribution or packaging. We knew of no storage of weapons and ammunition. We encouraged no extortion. We discouraged actively, twenty hours a day, the use of violent force to resolve conflict. I never had heard the name of the victim of a murder I was charged with helping to arrange until it was repeated to me by a reporter on the Friday when Mr. Rose made this charge last June.
>
> First let me suggest that the two principal witnesses who professed deep inside knowledge of the activities in First Church did not produce hard testimony. They did not specify dates nor

did they furnish corroborative detail. The charges were in terms of "always" and "lots of times."

In numerous searches of the building not so much as a milligram of marijuana was discovered or planted. No weapon was ever found hidden in the church by a Blackstone Ranger. No evidence of our having encouraged extortion or participated in planning violent acts was presented.

If the Chicago police can prove that we are guilty of crimes why haven't they brought us to trial? And if they do not have evidence of our guilt, then where, please, is our guilt if not in the overactive police imaginations?

On July 1, 1968, Jeff Fort, the leader of the Blackstone Rangers, was subpoenaed to testify at the Senate subcommittee on investigations. Fort appeared with his counsel, Marshall Patner. Patner stated to the committee that Fort wished the opportunity to cross-examine all witnesses who made statements tending to defame his character.

Senator McClellan, the chairman of the committee, refused to allow cross-examination of the witnesses; and Jeff Fort on advice of counsel refused to testify and walked out of the hearing. It was a dramatic and electrifying episode that burst upon the Chicago news media like a bombshell. The following is a record of the incident taken from the transcript of the hearings. It began with Patner's submitting the following statement:

My client, Mr. Jeff Fort, has been subpoenaed to appear before this committee concerning an investigation of the Woodlawn area Job Training Project, Chicago, Illinois, funded by the Office of Economic Opportunity. On behalf of Mr. Fort, I hereby request and demand:

1. That each person who has made statements or presented evidence before this subcommittee, either orally or in any written form, including by affidavit, which tends to defame Mr. Fort or otherwise adversely affects his reputation, and any persons who shall hereafter do so, be called to appear personally before Mr. Fort and his undersigned Counsel, after reasonable notice to Mr. Fort and said Counsel of the time and place of such personal appearance by each such person.
2. That the undersigned Counsel for Mr. Fort be permitted to personally orally cross-examine, in a reasonable manner, said persons described in paragraph 1, above.

THE CHAIRMAN: "Request number one is a matter that

addresses itself to the discretion of the committee, the number of witnesses to which you referred whose testimony may have reflected upon your client, Mr. Fort. A number of those witnesses have appeared in person, are here, some of them today in person, and as to whether the committee will call any other witnesses, witnesses that you may request, is a matter that addresses itself to the committee at the time you submit their names and make a special request for a given witness.

"Your request number two, that the undersigned counsel for Mr. Fort be permitted to personally orally cross-examine in a reasonable manner said persons described in paragraph one above cannot be granted under the Rules of the Committee.

"You may submit questions for the committee to present, to ask witnesses that may have appeared or may appear to testify with respect to your client.

"The committee will weigh those questions and if proper will ask the questions. . . ."

MR. PATNER: "It is our position that unless we are able to confront and cross-examine the witnesses, that we are denied any remedy to respond to the harm, that Rule 13 is not adequate to afford us a fair hearing. That rule should be amended, sir.

THE CHAIRMAN: "Well, that is your suggestion. You understand we have preferred no charges against your client. This is not a court. He is not on trial. This committee cannot deprive him of liberty or impose any penalty for anything he may have done.

"All this committee can do is to investigate matters that come within its jurisdiction which the Congress by appropriate resolution and by the rules of the Senate have instructed and given this committee a mandate to investigate and that is what we are doing. . . ."

MR. PATNER: "Senator Mundt and Mr. Chairman, as a great deal of the testimony, evidence, documents that have come in are based on hearsay, it is our position that it is inadequate that Mr. Fort defend himself from the charges that have been made unless he can confront and cross-examine those witnesses.

"Reserving all other questions that can be raised here ranging from the propriety of the subpoenaing and scope of the examination, we cannot proceed unless we can have the right to confront and cross-examine the witnesses."

TESTIMONY OF JEFF FORT, VICE PRESIDENT OF THE BLACKSTONE RANGERS (ACCOMPANIED BY COUNSEL: MARSHALL PATNER:)

THE CHAIRMAN: "Will you state your name—I have heard your statement—will you state your name, please?"

MR. FORT: "Jeff Fort."

THE CHAIRMAN: "Where do you live, Jeff?"
MR. PATNER: "I am sorry, Mr. Chairman, I must instruct my client we cannot participate without the right to cross-examine."
THE CHAIRMAN: "I am going to insist with the approval of the committee, the members present, two of which constitutes a quorum, that he answer the questions, and I will ask you to take your seat and have your client take his seat and let the questions be asked."
MR. PATNER: "I appreciate the courtesy, Mr. Chairman."
SENATOR MUNDT: "Mr. Chairman, before counsel speaks any further, I think he should be alerted to something he may not know. As far as I know, this may be your first appearance before the committee."
MR. PATNER: "Yes, sir."
SENATOR MUNDT: "There is only one manner in which your client can avoid testifying before this committee. He has the same right as any other citizen has: To take the Fifth Amendment on those questions which he thinks an honest answer might tend to incriminate him.

"If he simply refuses to answer the questions that you suggest he will be subject to a vote of contempt of Congress which provides a jail sentence of its own.

"I think you should know that. A lot of witnesses have walked out of this committee and other investigating committees and have wound up in the Federal jail because of the contempt of Congress. . . ."
MR. PATNER: "I appreciate Senator Mundt's admonition. It is our position that the hearing cannot be a fair one without the remedies and rights afforded that we have requested and reserving all other rights. I must advise my client that we cannot participate. Thank you sir."

(At this point Mr. Patner started to walk out along with his client.)
THE CHAIRMAN: "Just a moment. I don't think you want to show us a discourtesy."
MR. PATNER: "No, sir, I do not."
THE CHAIRMAN: "All right, be seated. Your client may be seated, also. Do I understand that you are advising your client, telling the committee and advising the client not to answer any questions that may be asked of him?"
MR. PATNER: "I am standing and advising my client to stand, Mr. Chairman, on the requests that we have made.

Unless those are granted so that we can have a fair hearing, we cannot participate."
THE CHAIRMAN: "I am asking you the question if you will permit your client to answer questions?"

MR. PATNER: "If those requests were granted he would answer all questions."
THE CHAIRMAN: "I have told you certain parts of your request will be considered in due course when the occasion arises for them. One of them will have to be denied under the Rules of the Committee."
MR. PATNER: "Yes, sir. It is upon the denial of that request that we cannot participate."
THE CHAIRMAN: "Your contention is because of denial of item number two you cannot proceed?"
MR. PATNER: "That is correct."
THE CHAIRMAN: "That is your statement. I am going to ask the questions and we will see whether he follows your advice. State your place of residence, Mr. Fort."
MR. PATNER: "Mr. Chairman, I am sorry, we cannot participate."
THE CHAIRMAN: "I don't need you to tell me at this time. I am going to ask the question."
MR. PATNER: "Can I answer the question? We cannot participate any further."
THE CHAIRMAN: "You are walking off refusing to let him testify?"
MR. PATNER: "On the conditions that I previously stated, Mr. Chairman."
THE CHAIRMAN: (raising his voice): "Will you not permit this committee to make a record by asking questions and letting him determine whether he will answer them or not?"
MR. PATNER: "The record is clear that he cannot testify on my advice."
THE CHAIRMAN: "Then I may say to you under these circumstances, as far as I know both of you are in contempt."

With that, Jeff Fort and his counsel withdrew from the hearing room amid the grinding of television cameras and the pandemonium that ensued as the working press followed them out for interviews. Several weeks later the full U.S. Senate voted to hold Jeff Fort in contempt of Congress.

The president of TWO was at last called to testify in defense of the efforts TWO had undertaken to work with alienated youth of the community. A week prior to giving this testimony the writer had received a call from Charles Percy, Republican Senator from Illinois, saying he would introduce him in the hearings and would remain with him throughout. He had made extensive inquiries into TWO and the youth project and had a deep concern for the work of TWO. This decision to take a public stand in support of the TWO president was courageous indeed. The hearings had been going on for more than two weeks, and practically all the news from them had cast the project in an unfavorable light. Many men holding public office would not have become involved.

Senator Percy's willingness to undertake an affirmative public stand on such a controversial issue is an indication of the depth of his conviction that new and creative ideas must be brought forth and implemented to help solve some of the complicated problems of the black ghetto, problems that have been created and exacerbated by a long history of racial discrimination and enforced segregation.

On the afternoon of July 1, Senator Percy and the writer entered the hearing room and took seats at the witness table. Senator Percy made the following remarks which have been taken from the hearing transcripts:

> THE CHAIRMAN: "Be seated. Senator Percy, the committee is glad to welcome you, sir. Do you have a statement you wish to make?"
>
> SENATOR PERCY: "Mr. Chairman, I appreciate very much the opportunity to appear before this sub-committee today and present to you one of my very distinguished constituents. The Reverend Arthur Brazier of the Apostolic Church of God located in the Woodlawn area is President of The Woodlawn Organization, and in that capacity is here to testify before the Permanent Sub-committee on Investigations.
>
> "Mr. Chairman, my introduction will be brief, because the Reverend Mr. Brazier has been waiting off and on for more than two weeks to present his testimony to you and I want you to have the maximum time possible to hear and question him. I do want to express to the committee my own interest in these hearings, and my desire—as a representative of the people in this area—to be helpful to the committee in any way I can in developing the facts surrounding this experimental grant by OEO to The Woodlawn Organization.
>
> "I am very anxious—as I know the Committee is—that all sides of the situation be explored fully so that an accurate picture of the validity of the project, in context of the area in which it is located, be fully presented in the course of the committee hearings. I sincerely hope that as the spotlight of public attention is focused on aspects of the program that allegedly have gone awry—or testimony on various unsavory activities

that are not a part of the project—it will be done in such a way that to persist in their work in these areas will not be deterred or discouraged.

"The work of the inner city is extremely high risk in nature. Often the failures outnumber the successes, and what successes there are seem almost invisible in relation to the magnitude of the problem.

"But nonetheless we must try. If ever we are going to cure these cancers of the cores of our older cities, we must persist. And we must give our sympathy and understanding to those courageous men and women who have turned their backs on far safer jobs to try to find the answers to the needs of these imprisoned persons of our slums and ghettos. . . .

"Accordingly, Mr. Chairman, I should like to present to the committee a list of six witnesses whose views—in addition to Rev. Brazier—I believe are essential to a full and fair presentation on the Woodlawn Project. These witnesses that I would suggest could be exceedingly helpful to the committee in the determination of a value judgment in this case would include, first, Alderman Leon Despres. He is the Democratic Alderman from the Woodlawn area. He has been the recipient of gang violence himself and is familiar with the relationship of the project to the Woodlawn community.

"Second, Dr. Julian Levi, Vice-President of the University of Chicago and Executive Director of the Southeast Chicago Commission. He is familiar with the relationship of the project to the community and familiar with the preliminary evaluation. In my judgment Dr. Julian Levi is one of the generally recognized most able and knowledgeable urban affairs experts in the country today.

"The third would be Mr. Ed Berry, Executive Director of the Chicago Urban League. The Urban League had the subcontract for generating job opportunities for the project and is therefore familiar with this aspect and the project generally.

"Fourth would be a representative from Xerox Corporation. Xerox Corporation has formulated and provided educational materials used in the project. Mr. Sam Sains, Xerox representative on the project in Chicago, is familiar with the teaching aspects of the project on a day-to-day basis.

"Fifth would be Dr. Harold Visotski, Director of the State Department of Mental Health, who served with great distinction under Governor Otto Kerner and who is very conversant with the general approach taken with the project but not with the particulars of the operation.

"Last, I recommend Senator Richard H. Newhaus, a Democrat, State Senator, former social worker. He represents the

Woodlawn-Hyde Park area and is conversant with the need for experimentation in projects of this kind.

"Today, I am personally introducing the Rev. Arthur Brazier because of my deep personal interest in the work he is doing, the community he is serving, and because of my high regard for his own personal integrity, selflessness, and courage.

"The Reverend Brazier is a man deeply concerned about the stability of his community. He has gathered considerable knowledge of juvenile delinquency and how to deal with it. The project that Woodlawn undertook for OEO is an experimental one in nature and is looked upon by him and the leadership of the Chicago community as a high risk venture.

"An official of the University of Chicago familiar with civic and urban affairs recently commented to me, 'If I were to name a half dozen of the most useful citizens in Chicago today, Reverend Brazier would certainly be among them.'

"This high regard is shared by a number of civic and business leaders who have worked with TWO and the Reverend Mr. Brazier, and who have written to me since the hearings started.

"The Rev. Mr. Brazier is realistic, hard-headed, and tough in his dealings with gang leadership. He has taken risks; I think he will agree he has made mistakes. But he has had some encouraging and some immensely successful results from the programs The Woodlawn Organization has undertaken through the years.

"I am pleased to present to you, Mr. Chairman, Rev. Brazier."

The following are excerpts from the statement prepared for the hearing.

REV. BRAZIER: "Mr. Chairman and distinguished Senators of this committee: As President of The Woodlawn Organization I welcome the opportunity to appear before this committee in order to express its sponsorship and participation in a program directed at the youth of our community. In sorrow we note that this program has not only been misunderstood and misinterpreted on occasion, but has also been a target of rumor and misrepresentation. Some background will be helpful.

"The Woodlawn Organization is a voluntary citizen's organization located on the Southeast side of the City of Chicago. The basic unit for membership and participation is the Block Clubs. In The Woodlawn Organization, we have approximately 90 Block Clubs and neighborhood associations. Our Block Clubs usually perform various services for their members. They are generally successful in involving all but the most personally disorganized individuals. All clubs answer pressing personal and collective needs.

"They bring pressure to bear upon slum landlords to maintain their buildings, they embark on clean-up campaigns, they demand city services such as garbage pickups and street and alley sweeping, they protest unfair police treatment, they also help residents get jobs or legal assistance or other personal services.

"Besides the Block Clubs, The Woodlawn Organization, known locally as TWO, has as part of its membership the two businessmen's associations in the area and groups from the established churches of Woodlawn whose denominations are: Baptist, Methodist, Episcopalian, Pentecostal, Lutheran, Roman Catholic and Presbyterian.

"Woodlawn is the unfortunate example of the deprived exploited Black Community, but without exception, the people, expressing themselves through TWO, are determined that the course of the development of their community be and remain in their hands. Our motto is "self-determination". The continued activities and existence of TWO is proof that this goal will be achieved.

"The committee, for instance, will be interested to know that TWO has been involved in several job training programs through which literally hundreds of people have received employment. The Woodlawn Organization, several years ago, interested a local foundation, the Kate Maremont Foundation, in joining with it in a joint partnership adventure to build new low-cost housing in the community. We formed a not-for-profit corporation known as the TWO-KMF Development Association and we have been awarded a nine-acre tract of land by the City of Chicago to build approximately 500 low-cost dwelling units to house some of the people of our community in decency and dignity.

"Now, the gang problem in Woodlawn is not a new one. As long ago as 1965 the police department of the City of Chicago and official youth welfare agencies were gathering statistics and data. As a matter of fact, on November 1, 1965, the Third Police District, in which Woodlawn is located, was sufficiently alarmed about the problem to prepare and circulate a catalogue of names, addresses, group affiliations, nick-names, and the like, running some 35 pages and including over 1,000 names. The sorry fact is, despite all of their efforts, the problem grew—it did not diminish. . . .

". . . The Woodlawn Organization came to the conclusion that something had to be attempted in order to preserve these young people and to save not only them and their families but society as well from what appeared to be inevitable results.

"We did so with full knowledge that any program aimed at juvenile delinquency control was a high risk venture; we knew that we were coming in after all of the official agencies had failed. We knew that we were dealing with young people who had been either pushed out, or dropped out of school. We knew that we would be dealing with young people whose attitudes and behavioral patterns were largely conditioned by the system of racial discrimination and segregation. We knew that we were handicapped with all of the inequities and deficiencies of public education, not only in the City of Chicago but elsewhere over the country. We knew that all of the known data indicated that great difficulties awaited us. . . .

"Considering the nature of the difficulties the community was experiencing with its youth, it was not at all surprising that a great number of young men brought into the program had police records, that was the purpose of the program. It would have been far easier to accept only youth with minor or unblemished records, only then, we would not have discharged our obligation.

"It is said that many of the young people that we took into the program got into trouble thereafter. Again, recognizing that after years of effort, the public authorities had failed to reduce the problem, and also that all prior experiences indicated a high degree of recidivism, this had to be expected.

"Nevertheless, records show that in the year prior to the institution of the program, that is from June 1, 1966, to May 13, 1967, there were 73 instances of gang-related shootings in the Woodlawn community in which 81 persons were shot. In the succeeding year, that is during the life of this program, there were 42 instances of gang-related shootings in which 50 persons were shot. A significant reduction.

"On the sad weekend following the assassination of Dr. Martin Luther King, acres of devastation developed from riots on the Westside of the City of Chicago, while in Woodlawn we had only 22 windows broken, two stores vandalized and one fire.

"Comparison of police statistics for the fourth period of 1968 shows increases in burglaries for the city as a whole of 69.3 percent as against a year earlier and for the troubled districts increases of 118 percent to 318 percent, whereas in Woodlawn the increase was only 49.2 percent. It has been said by some that the youth organizations extorted money from the businessmen during this period. The Woodlawn Businessmen's Association through newspapers and television denied this charge and wrote me a letter relative to it. . . . Further, it has been said that TWO was intimidated by the youth organizations. The truth of the matter is that these youth groups never, at any time, sought to intimidate The Woodlawn Organization and as a matter of fact when our investigations disclosed that a number of youths had given false information on their applications we removed more than 80 of them at one time from the program.

"It has been said that the project did not place enough of these young people on jobs. Part of our difficulty was in the continued criticism directed at the program by parts of the public press which frightened prospective employers and made our job that much more difficult. . . . In spite of this however, as of May 29, I have been informed by Mr. Anthony C. Gibbs, the Acting Project Director, that almost one hundred youths are now working on jobs and becoming productive citizens. In fact, one group of these young people working at the Atomic Commission's Argonne Laboratories now gets up at 5:30 every morning to go to work in a plant located some 30 miles from the city.

"It has been said that the program was wasteful. The Woodlawn Organization has not at any time knowingly wasted any federal funds. Our accounts have received a monthly review by Arthur Andersen and Company, a nationally known and respected auditing firm. It is difficult and often expensive to deal with these problems, but I would suggest that if we cannot deal with them this way, and in other innovative and creative ways, as taxpayers, we are going to have to pay for a generation of penitentiary and reformatory confinement together with all of the major costs of welfare and dependency.

"It has been said that the project paid inordinant numbers of sub-professionals, some of whom may have been in trouble with the law or even in jail. The policy of the project was never to pay anyone who was incarcerated. The project, however, was designed to use whatever skills and abilities we could find within the youth organizations. The social workers and youth workers all had their day. None have succeeded. We know that it is a high risk to take a youngster with a bad record and place confidence in him, but after all, repression had achieved nothing. We believe that the effort was justified.

"It has been said that the project never had an experienced director. This is true. There were 15 special conditions imposed upon us by Washington when this grant was established, one of which was that the Office of the Mayor would be invited to concur in the selection of a Project Director. Experienced persons with long records of success in the field of probation and job development were presented to the office of the Mayor and these persons never received concurrence from that office. In spite of this, The Woodlawn Organization's Youth Project made major contributions to the youth and to our community.

"Finally, the Youth Project in Woodlawn has been an attempt by the community and the devoted people in it to meet a tragic circumstance—created by generations of injustice, inequity and deprivation.

"That is the end of my statement, Mr. Chairman."

Following this testimony, the TWO president was questioned extensively by Senators McClellan, Mundt, and Curtis. It was their assessment that the program was a waste of government funds. There were other senators on the committee, however, who had a much more favorable assessment of the program and approached the situation in a real effort to get at the truth. Senators Jacob Javits of New York, Edwin Muskie of Maine, and Fred Harris of Oklahoma had a far deeper understanding of the problems we were trying to find solutions to; and they asked their questions in an impartial way so that the facts could be known.

It was clear to all observers, however, that due to the extreme pressure brought on by the Senate hearings OEO was not going to re-fund the youth project. It should be noted here that OEO had, over a long period of time, withstood tremendous pressure to close the project before its funding year was over. In spite of the pressure, OEO would not cut off the program funds but remained supportive to the end.

Bertrand M. Harding appeared before the Senate committee to testify concerning OEO's position relative to TWO's youth project. He had this to say in his opening statement:

> I welcome this opportunity to present the views of the Office of Economic Opportunity on the demonstration grant to The Woodlawn Organization in Chicago's Southside. Two basic issues are before us:
>
> 1. Should the Federal government try to salvage the hard-core alienated youth in our city slums; and
> 2. Was the Chicago pilot project a responsible attempt to get at this problem.
>
> I feel the answer is yes in both cases.

It is the writer's considered judgment that city hall deliberately killed the TWO youth demonstration project. This is not just one man's opinion. In an article in the *Chicago Daily News,* June 26, 1968, the same opinion is expressed:

> T.W.O. GANG PROJECT: DID IT FAIL?
>
> No Better and No Worse Than Other Such City Projects, Experts Say: Lack of Director Called Chief Handicap
>
> by Lois Wille
>
> The truth about the Woodlawn Organization's job-training project with the Blackstone Rangers, according to Chicago youth

workers and street-gang experts, is that it was no better and no worse than the city's other gang projects.

It ran into serious jams—but so have all the others.

"Gang work is a risky business," says Bruce Cole, divisional director of the program of the YMCA of Metropolitan Chicago, the city's most experienced youth agency.

"We've had youngsters in our program arrested and staff that got into difficulties, too. You try to sort it all out, and figure out where you went wrong.

"There is no way to play this game without hiring ex-convicts and some who are going to get into trouble again.

"And you have to give the kids some measure of control."

"Either the Senate committee doesn't understand what street-gang work is all about, or it is deliberately trying to make this one project look bad," said the director of one North Side youth agency.

"It could have been any of us up there before that committee."

NEVER HAD DIRECTOR

But the TWO project had one handicap the others don't have. It drifted through its nine-month course without a director. The Rev. Arthur M. Brazier, president of TWO, tried to double as project leader. He is considered an excellent community organizer and ran some successful job-training programs, but he had little experience working with street gangs.

The reason the project was leaderless is imbedded in Chicago politics, and in the hostility and mutual distrust between city officials, including the city antipoverty agency, and community organizations like TWO.

The OEO contract provided that Mayor Richard J. Daley was to "concur" with TWO in naming a director.

Last June, TWO's advisory committee, composed mainly of University of Chicago professors and welfare directors from private agencies, recommended an experienced New York gang worker and ex-probation officer. Daley rejected all of them.

SABOTAGE SUSPECTED

A University of Chicago professor active in Woodlawn welfare work and a consultant to several South Side welfare projects thinks the failure to hire a leader was a direct attempt by the city to sabotage the program.

"It was an effort to punish TWO, which has several times embarrassed Daley on urban renewal and school issues," he said.

Also, Daley has said that he disapproved of the way the project was funded. OEO awarded the grant directly to TWO, bypassing the city's antipoverty agency. The city agency had rejected a similar TWO proposal.

"The failure to get a director was the project's chief difficulty, the key to its troubles," the professor said. "It meant TWO had difficulty hiring professional teachers, and the staff in turn did not receive the assistance it should have had."

He listed several other shortcomings. "It lasted only from September through May, and was not full organized—if at all—until January. A project like this needs two years before it can show results.

"But if I had to make a judgment, from what I have seen in Woodlawn, I would say the project was very worthwhile."

ESTABLISHED PRACTICES

Most of the practices in the TWO project brought out in the Senate hearings were patterned after established, successful gang projects, according to youth workers. These included:

TWO worked within the gang structure, rather than trying to break up the gang. So do the city's other street-gang programs.

This shocked Sen. John L. McClellan (D.-Ark.), chairman of the Government Operations Committee's permanent subcommittee on investigations. "It reinforces crime," he said.

But the practice has been accepted here and in other cities for years, and now the trend is to let "reformed" gangs run their own projects.

LAST YEAR, for example, the West Side Vice Lords got $15,000 from the Rockefeller Foundation and $25,000 from the Field Foundation for an ice cream parlor and a landscaping program.

The Vice Lords prove the theory is valid, according to Cole. The YMCA first began working with them nearly 10 years ago, and for a number of years there has been very little Vice Lord criminal activity.

Police statistics in the Woodlawn area show that gang-inspired shooting incidents dropped 40 percent during the life of the TWO project, but gang workers think nine months was too short a time for lasting effect.

Dr. Irving Spergel was retained by the Office of Economic Opportunity to evaluate the program. Spergel is Professor and Chairman of Community Work Sequence, School of Social Service Administration, University of Chicago. He has written three books on delinquency: *Racketville, Slumtown, Haulburg; Street Gang Work;* and *Community Problem Solving: The Delinquent Example.* Spergel is generally recognized as an outstanding authority on street gang work. He had this to say about his experience in evaluating our project.

> We gathered four kinds of delinquency data related to the program: (1) Police District #3 Incident Data; (2) Police District #3 Juvenile Arrest Data; (3) The self-reports of participants in the program; and (4) Data on arrests of participants in the program derived from the newspapers. Comparisons were made of incidents and arrests the year prior to and the year during the operation of the program. In almost every major category, the findings are consistent and conclusive that the incidents of crime and arrests declined absolutely or relative to other comparable areas in the city and the city as a whole. The only exception was the category of murder and manslaughter. It should be noted that the figures in this category are quite small and, furthermore, that murder and manslaughter tend ordinarily not to be a product of gang warfare.
>
> Because of the failure of the Chicago Police Department to cooperate with the researcher in the provision of arrest data on individuals in the program, a full analysis of the impact of the program on delinquency is not possible. Nevertheless, there remains an extremely high probability that the program was instrumental in lowering delinquency in the district.
>
> I have no question that the program should have been extended. Certainly, a great many young people were involved in the program. There was clear evidence of delinquent reduction, which is probably a result of the program. There was evidence of job placement.
>
> It is difficult to come to any conclusion about the Program failures; the basic failure of the program was essentially political. The program was not able to develop fully because of political opposition. The kind of programmatic evaluation that we are writing is really of secondary importance. The political factors primarily determined the life and particularly the death of the program. The basic political issue was who would control the program.
>
> There are some specific program defects, however: (1) A lack of professional personnel; (2) a lack of sufficient lead-up time in the training of nonprofessionals; (3) the lack of certain community support structures, particularly from agencies, which was not possible because of political pressures; and (4) there were also some flaws in the basic design of program. Certain expected outcomes were not realistic; others should have been stated and were not.

The Woodlawn Organization's dramatic and significant effort to meet the needs of our community's out-of-school alienated youth ended here. The project was killed because the political establishment could not tolerate an independent community organization such as TWO receiving federal funds that were not controlled by the Establishment itself. The project was killed because white society refused to permit the indigenous leaders in the black ghetto to deal with problems of alienated youth—a problem that white society itself by its indifference and racism has forced on the ghetto.

Chapter Ten

The Uses of Power and the Role of the Church

Many people are unconcerned with the biblical justification for the use of power, but for Christians this is an important consideration. This chapter will look at two problems: a biblical justification for the use of power, and the role of the church in the status quo.

Some people fear the word "power" has an evil connotation, that power is demonic and somehow corrupts men, and especially that a power-based organization is not consistent with biblical teaching. This writer is convinced that power in and of itself does not corrupt. The wrong use of power corrupts, but the right use of power is consistent with the Bible. God uses power in a variety of ways to bring about his program, and he has given man dominion over the earth—power, if you will—personal as well as social.

God in his creative power demonstrated that he is the source of all power. The Bible tells that at a point of his own choosing God created the heavens and the earth. The power brought to bear transcends human thought and imagination, for God spoke and creation took place. God said, "Let there be light," and there was light. God said, "Let there be a firmament in the midst of the waters," and it was so. Again God said, "Let the waters under the heavens be gathered into one place and let the dry land appear," and it was so. In the greatest creative act of all God said, "Let us make man in our own image . . . and let them have dominion over all the earth."

In creation we see God's direct power. In redemption we see God acting powerfully through an agent. In the book of Exodus that agent is Moses. God confronted Moses in a Midianite field and gave him what seemed to be an impossible charge. He told Moses, no longer a young man eager for conflict, a refugee from Pharaoh's court keeping sheep for his father-in-law, to go back to Egypt, to confront mighty Pharaoh, and to bring the people of Israel out from slavery.

In a series of confrontations with Pharaoh, Moses made eight demands, each the same as the last: This is a message from the Lord God of Israel—let my people go. Pharaoh reacted to this demand as all people have reacted who want to maintain the status quo. He resisted. Pharaoh, in his arrogance, said he knew nothing of the Lord, and he would not let Israel go.

After that direct confrontation the battle was joined, and it took ten judgments before Pharaoh yielded and let the people of Israel go. The tenth and final judgment was the worst of all—the death of all the firstborn of the Egyptians. With this final show of power, Pharaoh's resistance was broken and he consented to release the children of Israel from their bitter bondage. It is clear in the book of Exodus that God through Moses exercised power in a most dynamic and positive way in redeeming the people of Israel from their bondage in the land of Egypt.

Nothing happens in a vacuum. There has to be a historical vehicle through which all circumstances operate. In the New Testament, for instance, we read of God's using the power of Caesar to fulfill the prophetic announcement that Christ would be born in Bethlehem. Caesar Augustus decreed that a census should be taken and that every man had to go to his home town and register there. Since Bethelehem was the city of Joseph's ancestors, Joseph and Mary traveled from their home in Nazareth to Bethlehem, and Jesus was born while they were there. God used the power of Caesar in a political event—another example of the role of power in history—to make a decree that forced people to do his will.

Now let us look at another kind of power: the power of John the Baptist. This was not a weak and timid individual, but a dynamic and powerful personality. John, through his dynamism and power—not the power of violence, but the power of prophetic speech—attracted huge throngs. The people represented potential social power. John was so effective that many of the religious leaders were forced to come out of the city of Jerusalem to the Jordan River in the wilderness to hear what he had to say, to see if he was a threat to the status quo.

Here is a power mechanism being brought into play to set the stage for the beginning ministry of Jesus. At the height of John's power as a preacher, Jesus appeared on the scene. John announced to the crowd of people standing about him, "Look! There comes the Lamb of God who is taking away the sin of the world." John's followers soon became Jesus' followers. Jesus had a ready-made following, a "power base," when he began his ministry.

Both civil power and religious power were used in relation to Jesus, the civil power in terms of the census being taken, and the religious power in John the Baptist's preaching and baptizing. God, in bringing about his purposes, used both civil and religious power.

This idea is hard for some people to accept because they believe God does not act outside the religious structure. God did act outside the religious structure in the census decree. In the Old Testament also, Jeremiah called Nebuchadnezzar, the tyrannical king of Babylon, God's servant, whom he would bring to punish Israel for her idolatry and her unjust oppression of the poor.

We see God's power in the Gospels in the life of Jesus Christ, who was both God and man. Christ was not a demigod, half God and half man. He was all truly God and truly man. People today accept rather easily the fact of Jesus as a man. He was also God, however, and as God he exercised prerogatives of deity. He even forgave sins. The scribes and the Pharisees accused him of blasphemy when he forgave the sins of a paralyzed man, because they knew that only God can forgive sins.

Jesus demonstrated that he was God by exercising power over nature. A great storm arose when he was in a ship with his disciples. The ship was filling with water, and they were in danger of sinking. Jesus, who was asleep in the ship, was aroused by the frantic cries of his disciples. He awoke and commanded the wind and the sea to be still, and they were still.

He exercised power over disease. Wherever Jesus went he healed the lepers, the crippled, the blind among those crowds that gathered and followed him.

Jesus exercised power over demons. Mark tells us of a man

possessed by demons who gave every appearance of being a maniac. He lived among the tombs, and although he had been chained he broke the chains and menaced passers-by. Jesus sent the demons out of him. When the people heard of the incident and came out to see for themselves, they found the man who had been a raving maniac, sitting fully clothed and in his right mind.

Jesus exercised power over death. The story of the raising of Lazarus vividly illustrates this point. Martha and Mary, the sisters of Lazarus, told Jesus that Lazarus was dead and buried and his body was decaying. Jesus went to the grave of Lazarus and commanded some of the followers to remove the stone that lay upon the grave. He called to Lazarus to come forth. John tells us that the man who had been dead came forth, still bound with grave clothes, and with a cloth around his face. Jesus told them to unbind him and let him go free.

In order for Jesus to demonstrate complete power over death, however, he must be able to raise from the dead one who would never die again. This Jesus stated he had power to do in the sixth chapter of the Gospel of John. "And this is the will of my father, that everyone who sees the Son and believes on him should have eternal life; and I will raise him up at the last day."

These examples of the uses of power show that the possession of power is not, in itself, an evil thing. It is how that power is used that must concern us. Power has been and can continue to be used for good.

Rather early in his ministry, Jesus began to advance the claim that he was the Messiah. He could not possibly have been accepted as Messiah, however, merely by advancing the claim. It is common practice, even today, for persons to present proof of their identity. A man must present papers of identification to cash a check at a bank where he is unknown. A credit card or driver's license indicates that he is the person he claims to be. In the same way Jesus had to present credentials that would establish the claim that he was the Messiah. His credentials were his power-demonstrating acts. He used his power not in wild, magical demonstrations designed to cause his followers to gaze and wonder, but in constructive ways to aid the poor, the oppressed, the sick. He used his power to heal the sick, to open the eyes of the blind, to make the lame walk, to cleanse the lepers, and to raise the dead. These were his credentials—his demonstration that he was the Messiah.

We see Jesus exercising his power in another way, a way much more aggressive and disturbing to the religious power structure. Mark tells us that Jesus went into the temple and sent out people who sold and bought things to sacrifice in the temple. He also upset the tables of the moneychangers and the dove sellers. It appears that in some fashion Jesus exercised control over the temple precincts, for Mark goes on to say that he would not permit any man to carry anything through the temple. This act turned the scribes and chief priests completely against Jesus, and they began to plot his death. Jesus' power and influence among the people was growing, and this the religious leaders could not tolerate.

Now, let us note Jesus' tactics. When he came he did not make an appeal to the monied interest. He did not go to the people in power and plead with them to do the right thing on the basis of morality. He went to the poor. He did not talk to them about personal salvation only. He dealt first with what the poor considered to be real in their lives. He dealt with their sickness, their leprosy, blindness, hunger.

The religious leaders who were in authority wanted to kill Jesus. The Scriptures make it very clear, however, that they were not able to do anything to him because of their fear of the people. Jesus built a mass base of people-power with which the religious leaders had to reckon.

Jesus' ministry was a demonstration of power, and this power threatened to change the status quo. It was this threat to the status quo of the power structure that was the catalyst, from the human point of view, that brought about his death.

The Wrong Uses of Power

The arrest and subsequent crucifixion of Jesus was a wrong use of power, by both the religious authorities and the secular authorities. He was arrested at night, moved from place to place in rapid succession because the authorities feared the people. In a short period of time, he underwent five trials—two before the Sanhedrin, the religious ruling body; two before Pontius Pilate, the Roman governor; one before King Herod. False witnesses were secured and paid to perjure themselves.

The religious leaders condemned him and turned him over to Pontius Pilate to be put to death. The Jews would have put him to death themselves had the power resided in their hands. This death penalty rested in the hands of the civil rulers. Pontius Pilate used his power wrongfully, for he ordered the crucifixion of Jesus even when he himself had said he found no fault in him.

Some of those in authority in the very earliest period of the gathered believers were putting their power to wrong use by discriminating against one group of widows. The book of Acts records that there was a disagreement between those of them who spoke Greek and those who spoke Hebrew. The former group complained that their widows were being overlooked in the daily distribution of food. The apostles did not try to refute this complaint. They realized the wrong use of power and they acted to change the manner of distribution. They asked the disciples to choose from among themselves seven men of good character to take on this work of services while the apostles themselves went on with the work of preaching and teaching.

In the centuries between the early church and today, men in power positions often used their power wrongfully for various reasons. In the middle sixteenth century the hierarchy of the church used its power to stifle dissent. One of the Augustinian priests, Martin Luther, after years of agonizing with his own conscience, developed certain strong religious convictions that were at odds with the doctrines of the Roman Catholic Church at that time. He felt very strongly the biblical truth of these convictions and felt they should be made public and be the subject of open debate. Instead, however, Luther was badgered by John Eck until he asserted biblical authority over papal and conciliar authority. He was then called a heretic, forced to undergo a heresy trial, and excommunicated.

In the eleventh century the long struggle between Pope Gregory VII and Emperor Henry IV over secular investiture of church officials illustrates another wrong use of power. The pope wanted to smash his opposition instead of recognizing the valid interests of his opponent and working with him. When Henry insisted on his right to choose and grant authority to bishops, that claim ran directly against the Pope's interests, so the Pope used his power of excommunication to bring Henry to heel.

In the sixteenth century John Calvin, in his second stay in Geneva, used the power of his office to cut down a man who criticized him personally as a minister. Calvin responded by saying the man had attacked his office, and humiliated him by making him walk through the streets with a sign around his neck. In the same way both politicians and civil rights leaders sometimes respond to a personal attack as if their position rather than some personal weakness were under criticism.

In the nineteenth century, Trinity Church in New York used economic power not only to amass wealth at the expense of the poverty-stricken tenants in church-owned tenements, but also to oppose laws that called for improvement in this kind of housing.

Ministers in Little Rock, Arkansas in this century used their eccelesiastical power to maintain the institution of segregation by preaching against the philosophy of integration and by teaching their parishioners that this was condoned and even spelled out in the Bible. Some ministers and church leaders who did not feel the Bible taught such a thing remained silent, and this silence was taken for sanction.

These are instances of the wrong use of power throughout history—both within and outside the church.

The Role of the Church in the Status Quo

Both clergy and laity have engaged in a great deal of discussion concerning the role of the church in civil rights movements and in the struggle for power of the minority groups. Should the church be involved in civil rights movements? Should the church participate in attempts to change the status quo toward a more favorable balance for the poverty-stricken, the disadvantaged, the oppressed people?

Becoming involved in civil rights movements is a matter of tactics, and could be answered Yes or No depending on the circumstances of a given congregation or denomination. It depends on how they can be most effective. For example, one church group might be more effective by working first on its own attitudes toward racial issues and minority groups rather than becoming involved in civil rights movements. Another group might be ready to become directly involved in marches, protests, voter registration, and other activities making up civil rights movements.

Attempting to change the oppressive status quo, however, is a matter not of tactics but of principle. There is no way to avoid or postpone answering these questions, because at a fundamental level every church is participating all the time in the oppressive status quo, either to change it or to uphold it or some mixture of the two. Since at this moment in history the Christian church as an institution is inextricably bound up with other social structures and institutions, it is maintaining the oppressive status quo unless it makes strenuous efforts to take the side of those who are trying to upset it for the sake of those who suffer under it. That is to say, if the church does nothing whatsoever, and remains perfectly neutral, it will still be favoring the situation in this country as it is, including white racism. There is no possibility of not acting or not taking sides when it comes to the matter of the status quo.

Some clergy and laity still say that the only concern of the church must be to "preach the gospel." People who take this position seem to view man as two separate and distinct entities—soul and body. They advance the idea that the church's role is to work with the soul of man, to work for his eternal salvation. They feel it is the duty of the secular agencies of our society to provide for a man's material needs. By their very withdrawal from the affairs of society such people effectually uphold and perpetuate the status quo.

Scripture, however, shows that the body and soul are inseparable. It is forcefully implied in the Scriptures that the soul cannot be dealt with as a separate entity divorced from the body.

The apostle Paul, writing to the Thessalonians, showed his concern for the whole man when he prayed for the well-being of their bodies as well as for their souls and spirits (I Thess. 5:23).

Church members will contribute money to support missionary hospitals and schools in foreign countries. They know that in order to reach the people of the foreign lands to which they have sent their missionaries, they must do something to change the wretched and miserable conditions of the life of the people. Missionaries do not wait for a man's soul to be saved first. They try to give people better nourishment, better education, better medical care *along with the gospel,* lest the preaching of the gospel become irrelevant and the grace of God obscure. Missionaries involve themselves in the total life of the people with whom they are working for the sake of Christ.

Why is it that some church members while supporting total involvement abroad oppose total involvement at home? There are probably several reasons. First, some Christians are overcharged with the utopian idea that, "If we preach the gospel, we change the hearts of all men and then we will all love one another and our problems will be solved." This apparently automatic and effortless evolvement of a society built on love of each person for the other finds no support in the New Testament. Even the apostle Paul had to struggle continuously with the evil in his own heart. He also worked untiringly with his fellow believers to help them do the same. The baneful effects of the evil in the hearts of men stand as a constant challenge to the beneficial effects of the grace of God shown in the gospel.

Second, these Christians feel this life is not important, that only heaven is. A study of Scripture will show how much of biblical teaching speaks to living here and now, highlighted against a setting of history that is moving toward completion and Christ's coming again.

But there is more. The virus of racism has so deeply infected our national life that it has also invaded the stronghold of the gospel—our churches—and poisoned the minds of Christians. It is understandable, but not excusable, that Christians would be caught up in the countless manifestations of racism that pervade American life. The depth and extent of racism in society is just now beginning to trickle into the consciousness of white society. The Christian church as an institution shares that racism, which is founded upon a fundamental misconception that whites are superior to blacks, and is built up with all the diabolical permutations and convolutions that spring from the minds of men who accept such a false premise.

The New Testament sets out clearly a position of equality when it unequivocally states that none of the biological, ethnic, social, or psychological distinctions by which we compartmentalize men and make some inferior and some superior has any validity as far as their standing before God in Christ is concerned (cf. Col. 3:11). If this is the case, then surely there can be no such artificial distinction and barrier in our relationship with each other.

Many church members have used the power of the church to maintain the status quo of segregation, suppression, and poverty. They say that the church ought not become involved in what they call social issues. They know that the church, if it becomes involved with the struggle of the black man for freedom and equality, will force many changes to be made in society. They are reluctant to see these changes because they threaten their security and their so-called American way of life. Sometimes these same people label Communistic or un-American efforts to open to the black man equal opportunity in jobs, housing, and education.

Many denominations, on the other hand, have taken an official position that discrimination and segregation because of race is un-Christian and sinful. Several of these official statements are quoted below:

> *Church of the Brethren*
> We affirm our belief that discrimination owing to color is out of keeping both with the teachings of the New Testament and with the stated position of the church of the Brethren.
>
> *Disciples of Christ*
> Whereas the denial of any of these inalienable rights of men and nations is a denial of the Christian gospel in that it strikes at the nature of God, and, thus, the nature of man . . . be it resolved: First—that we urge and encourage all ministers and churches of our communion to be willing to bear any cross of persecution or reprisal upon them by their fearless witness to the rights of all people, regardless of race or ethnic origin, to liberty, equality, justice and human dignity, and to the true nature of the church and the proclamation of the gospel of Christ without fear of favor.
>
> *Methodist Bodies*
> The position of the Methodist Church, long held and frequently declared, is an amplification of our Lord's teaching. To discriminate against a person solely upon the basis of his race is both unfair and unchristian. Every child of God is entitled to that place in society which he has won by his industry and his character. To deny him that position of honor because of the accident of his birth is neither honest democracy or good religion. . . . There must be no place in the Methodist Church for racial discrimination or enforced segregation.

> *Presbyterian Bodies*
> As Christians we hold that all forms of racial discrimination and segregation are denials of human worth and are contrary to the will of God.

Many other denominations have taken the position that segregation and discrimination based on race or ethnic background is out of harmony with their official religious positions. In the light of the official stand of the denominations it is imperative that the churches move forcefully in the direction of bringing their considerable power and influence to bear to correct the evils that have sprung from segregation and discrimination. We have a situation in our cities that is a shame before God and man. Millions of people have been systematically disenfranchised by effective conspiracies. Black people have been systematically denied education and the ability to earn a living.

One common argument runs thus: "There are more opportunities now for Negroes than ever before." That there are more opportunities today does not in any way negate the fact that millions of people are now suffering because of the restrictions imposed upon them. We cannot say, "Let's forget about the problem because things are somewhat better now." Black society will need *special* opportunities for many years to overcome the long period of injustice and degradation heaped upon the black man in this country, which has resulted in hopelessness and fear.

How does the clergyman's life of faith tie in with this biblical discussion? The personal philosophy and faith of the writer rests in part upon the words of the Lord Jesus, who said, "Love your neighbor as yourself." The question of who my neighbor is arose from this statement, and out of that question the Lord gave us the parable of the Good Samaritan.

If a modern-day clergyman goes out into the larger community he sees the slums in which many people are forced to live, the conditions under which they exist. He sees the abysmal education that hundreds of black children receive, the soaring crime rates in black ghetto areas, the poor health and sanitation conditions, the higher incidence of major disease with the lower availability of medical service in the ghetto. He sees the inadequate garbage collection, the exploitation of ghetto residents by local merchants. If he closes his eyes to the means whereby black people can help themselves he is as guilty as the priest or Levite of the parable. If he says, "I have nothing to do with this social problem; I am only here to preach the gospel," he quite effectively passes by on the other side. The two persons best able to have come to the aid of the hurt man on the Jericho road, the priest and the Levite, did not; and the man least expected to give aid was the one who helped.

There is a parallel to this in society today. The lead in obliterating from our society the injustice and discrimination is not coming primarily from the religious world, but from the secular state. The U.S. Supreme Court came to grips with an issue that has both moral and legal ramifications. The Supreme Court dealt with the legal issue and ruled that segregation and discrimination based on color was unconstitutional. The church should have led the way and dealt with the moral issue as well.

Any church, whether it be Baptist, Pentecostal, Methodist, Catholic, that gives support to the immoral system of repression, by silence or by saying, "Our role is to preach the gospel and to save souls only," is denying Christ and his clear teaching and example. The church can lead the way in changing the status quo, or by silence she can join the forces of oppression.

Afterword

A Call for Black Solidarity

These are truly solemn times—times of anxiety, uncertainty, and intense emotions, times of blurred and confused goals. These are times of frustration and uncertainty for even the most experienced among us. For the powerless black men and women who have not experienced the power of unity, these are times of absolute bewilderment.

The urgency of this moment in history cannot be stressed too much. For those whose contact with the world of the black ghetto is mainly via the mass media, the situation may seem to be settling down. But within the ghetto itself, poverty, injustice, hatred and despair are as harshly real as ever. Once again western civilization is being called upon to choose between fascism and freedom. Certain powerful sections of the established order are making it candidly clear that they prefer the facism of a police state to a freedom that includes black people. Nations such as the Union of South Africa and Rhodesia make no bones about where they stand, but some others are a little less blunt. They use the language of freedom while employing the tactics of fascism. Some hide behind such slogans as "property rights," while others use the bed sheet of "law and order."

The situation would not be so serious if it involved only a handful of fanatics waving Nazi banners and spouting racist slogans, but that is not the case. Today's brand of racism is much more subtle than that. In the South, in the North, the East, the West, and certainly in the Midwest, racism is present, aided by some of the nation's most powerful political leaders: congressmen, senators, aldermen, ward committeemen, police officers, both big and small industrialists, educators, newspaper publishers, TV and radio station owners, churchmen, educators, lawyers. The virus of racism is so strong that it has to some degree permeated all these areas of national life. Most of these people would never consider themselves racists, but acting out of self-interest and a lack of compassionate understanding, they carry out or aid racist designs.

The central purpose of this book is to urge and to plead for immediate action and a visible strategy to promote the security and solidarity of black people in Woodlawn and throughout the nation. It is an appeal for a truly genuine, unbreechable racial solidarity plus a racial stategy that is workable and makes sense. I emphasize solidarity and strategy because without them, we can forget about any kind of security.

When newspaper columnists say that we are living in critical times, it is a gross understatement. Black people must realize that we are at this moment in the midst of a life-or-death struggle for human dignity and survival. We are near the big showdown for the future of freedom and democracy in this country. Millions of white Americans have called for this showdown. A brief era of "liberal" concern seems largely to have given way to the old racism, though now it is seldom expressed as blatantly as it once was. White people have grown tired of hearing about their own racism; they have lost patience with black demands; they feel threatened by black progress. Thus they have closed their eyes once again to the crying needs of the black ghetto; or worse, they have actively opposed the black quest for tangible equality.

In 1877 the racist of the South and the racist of the North got together and brought an end to the Reconstruction Era—virtually wiping out all the gains won following the Civil War. That year marked the beginning of a new kind of slavery in the United States. Is it possible that yet another kind of slavery is in store for black men and women right here in this last half of the twentieth century?

I believe there are two basic conditions that must obtain before there can be slavery. First, there must be people who want to enslave other people, and second, there must be people who want to be slaves. I refuse to establish the latter condition, because I know that black people reject slavery—and I mean slavery in any form, including plantation politics, inferior schools, inferior housing, inferior employment, inferior public services, and—let us never forget—*absentee control of our communities.* We all should make a thorough study of the history of American slavery because it is most instructive. It has a direct bearing on the racism of today. In many ways it explains the efforts to destroy TWO; it explains the assassination of Dr. Martin Luther King, Medgar Evars, all the other martyrs—both white and black—of the civil rights movement.

While the propagandists for slavery tried to prove that our black ancestors were happy under slavery, they knew that the hunger for freedom was so strong they could not risk the successful rebellion or escape of a single black slave. That is the reason behind the fugitive slave law, the reason for the public exposure of every caught runaway slave to extreme torture and punishment, the reason it was necessary to punish and threaten—if not destroy—every white person who would assist in any uprising or escape.

They knew that freedom is a contagious thing. They knew that freedom has the power to excite imitation and mass emulation. Let one black man or woman stand up and assert his humanity, then he or she is certain to incite others—if they get away with it. In order to maintain slavery, the slavocracy and its friends instituted every form of legal, psychological, and physical instrument known to man—including the church.

The same frame of mind prevails today. The new slavocracy must squelch the black revolution. It must destroy its true leaders, and in the case of rebellious community movements, capture them and place them under lock and key, subject them to public torture and punishment. If they do not do this, others will be inspired by the success of any one great movement. They subjected TWO to all sorts of public torture and punishment, but we refused to die. We refused to give in. The black revolution in Woodlawn is still on. But more than Woodlawn is at stake.

The core of TWO's program is SELF-DETERMINATION FOR BLACK PEOPLE. That is the bone of contention. That is why TWO is considered a staunch enemy of racism in Chicago.

There is a scientific logic to the madness so rampant in racist Chicago. Enemies of democracy have been studying the population figures of the past two decades, and what they see they do not like. In a few decades black people will be the majority in Chicago.

An ever swelling black urban population coupled with a steady exodus of whites to the suburbs produces a rather strange phenomenon, one worthy of serious research by a high-powered board of psychiatrists and economists. The alarmed white racist could easily solve his problem by not running at the sight of the first black man to move into his neighborhood. But he wants to have his cake and eat it too. His strategy is to run from the city, down expensive expressways built by public funds, and then control the city from his estate in the suburbs or on the far outskirts of town. This is what has happened with the old neighborhoods. This is the story of the absentee landlord. This is the story of the ward-committeeman living on the Gold Coast while controlling an all-black community. This is the story of Uncle Tom overseers keeping the ward quiet for the white boss.

But it is another story when a community has self-determination is the same as it is toward freedom: it is simply of the citizens of Woodlawn: this is the crisis of every black community in Chicago. This is the problem of black America, because as of 1960, over 73 percent of black America lives in an urban society. If TWO wins the self-determination struggle here in Woodlawn it will lift the spirits, rekindle the fires of self-respect and dignity of all black Americans.

I do not accuse the white power structure of being against self-determination. They are for self-determination in their own communities. They are for it everywhere the overwhelming majority of the community is white. Their attitude toward self-determination is the same as it is toward freedom: it is simply wonderful—except for black people.

Black people need self-determination not only out of sheer self-respect; it is a dire necessity. Despite all the gains we have made through national legislation, decisions by the Supreme Court, and a change of attitude on the part of a few white Americans; despite all the marching, the protesting, the bloodshed, the assassinations and imprisonments, the black man in America is in dire straits. All of the sins of 350 years of subjugation, combined with all the obstructive forces of a neofascism in America, continue to take their toll of black bodies and souls.

We are still at the bottom of the totem pole in every facet of human existence with the exception of SOUL. But with Soul we must add solidarity and we must make that solidarity mean something, by giving it a strategy that makes sense to the black community. Simply making an emotional speech denouncing "Whitey" is not a strategy. Announcing plans to go back to Africa is not a strategy. Telling people not to participate in politics, not to vote in a particular election, is not really a strategy. I, as one man, will not attempt to play God and tell black people what the strategy should be. From now on, any strategy that we pursue should represent the opinions, thoughts, insights and experiences of a large number of black people, not just a few who happen to hold office at the top. We must discontinue the nationwide practice of allowing a few people to set national black policy off the top of their heads. We must stop basing our programs on ad hoc decisions that respond only to some crisis of the moment.

From this moment on, we must understand that we are in a war against extinction. Call it a struggle against genocide and suicide if you will, but do not understate the plight of the black man. We are in trouble, and because of its long history of racist habits, this whole nation is in trouble. We of TWO cannot solve the problems of the nation, but we can set an example of black people in a disadvantaged community asserting their humanity with solidarity.

We really have no alternative. Either we establish community power or we shall forever remain at the mercy of poverty, poor housing, inadequate education, and joblessness. If there are those who believe that remaining silent on these crucial issues will make the white backlash treat us a little better, permit me again to reflect back on history. It was in September of 1896 that Booker T. Washington made his Atlanta Compromise speech, in which he announced a new policy of accommodation for black people. The white newspapers and big-money men made him the new spokesman for the black freedom seeker. They were impressed that Washington advised his people not to seek their rights aggressively on the political and civil fronts and to nullify their quest for social equality. In his famous speech he said, "Cast down your buckets where you are," implying that they would get fresh water. In answer to Booker T. Washington's compromise oration, the racist rewarded the black American with a long-sustained system of law by terror, lynchings, abuse, and the denial of nearly all human rights. Lerone Bennett in his book *Before the Mayflower* said, "Down went the buckets and up they came filled with brine." The truth is that we have had more terror and violence in years prior to the black revolution than anything witnessed in recent years. The big difference is that not enough people cared to have it publicized and we did not have television—and above all, there were not enough people—including black people—who stood up to say, No more!

This is a great, challenging moment in the lives of black people, but it is not new for us. We have experienced such moments before—many times before in our history. Let us remember just who we are: we are the descendants of great men and women of courage and dignity; we are the descendants of Crispus Attucks, Nat Turner, Denmark Vesey, and the great Cinque, who started a black revolt before he reached American shores by capturing the slave traders' ship and steering it to shore. Our heritage is the heritage left by Harriet Tubman, Sojourner Truth, Frederick Douglass, and the nearly 200,000 Blacks who fought valiantly in the Civil War. Our heritage is the soul of every black man and woman who said NO to slavery.

We want the racists and all their bedfellows to know that we are not going to run away from this land, which was made great by the blood and sweat of our forefathers, long before today's racists came to this country. While seeking self-determination we are not calling for a self-imposed segregation. This is the land of Jean Baptiste DuSable, and we shall insist upon the right to live, work, go to school and play anywhere we can afford. We resist now and we shall continue to resist this land's vicious policy of housing, school, and job discrimination.

We must unite. We must consolidate; we must get our minds, our souls, our bodies, our money, and our energies *together*. We simply cannot permit the disintegration of the black revolution. Our new solidarity should not be based on personal feelings and past disagreements. At this moment of history, we cannot afford to dislike anybody who is for the freedom and self-determination of Black America.

In this call for black unity I do not preclude the support of white Americans for freedom. We must not fall into the same racist trap that has warped the minds of so many white Americans. Not all white people are racists, just as not all Negroes are a part of the black freedom movement.

This book has tried to say one thing above all: The black freedom movement must be formulated, directed, and led by black people. Black men must demand freedom and self-determination, and struggle together to get them. One of the greatest men ever produced at any time in this country, Frederick Douglass, said: *If there is no struggle, there is no progress. Those who profess to favor freedom, and yet deprecate agitation, are men who want crops without plowing up the ground. They want rain without thunder and lighting. They want the ocean without the awful roar of its many waters. This struggle may be a moral one; or it may be a physical one; or it may be both moral and physical; but it must be a struggle. Power concedes nothing without a demand. It never did and never will. . . .*

Douglass was speaking about black leadership, black solidarity, black strategy, black security, black progress, and black freedom with dignity: in short, black self-determination.

Index